Hellbent for Enlightenment

Hellbent for Enlightenment

Unmasking Sex, Power, and Death with a Notorious Master

ROSEMARY HAMILTON

WHITE CLOUD PRESS
ASHLAND, OREGON

Printed in Canada

01 00 99 98   5 4 3 2 1

Photography credits:
Grateful acknowledgment to Osho International Foundation (Poona, India) for the use of photographs in this book.

LIBRARY OF CONGRESS CATALOGING-IN-PUBLICATION DATA

Hamilton, Rosemary, 1923-
    Hellbent for enlightenment : unmasking sex, power, and death with a
  notorious master / Rosemary Hamilton
              p.   cm.
    ISBN 1-883991-15-3
    1. Hamilton, Rosemary, 1923-   . 2. Rajneesh, Bhagwan Shree, 1931-1990.
    3. Rajneeshees--Oregon--Rajneeshpuram--Biography.
    4. Rajneesh Foundation International--Controversial literature.
    I. Title.
    BP605.R344H36   1998
    299' .93--dc21
    [B]   98-12238
                                                    CIP

Table of Contents

Note to the Reader

Here is the story of my life with Osho. It is written without diary from memories rekindled and fanned by many fellow sannyasins. I have set down these memories in patterns rather than in sequence, following real life, where events from the past often bubble up to shed light on the present.

But many mystics, including Christ and Buddha, Socrates, Zen masters and Osho, insist that this "real" life of ours is not really real. They tell us that our authentic life is inner, and the inner world is timeless. We are urged to wake up, to live in this moment. The frequent use of present tense in the book is to convey this sense of urgency, of immediacy.

So if now and then you wonder what time belt we're in, not to worry. Consider these words from Rodgers and Hart's immortal love song. Any seeker who has fallen in love with a real master will sing "Amen":

> *I didn't know what time it was;*
> *Then I met you.*
> *Oh what a lovely time it was,*
> *How sublime it was, too.*
>
> *I didn't know what year it was;*
> *Life was no prize.*
> *I wanted love—and here it was*
> *Shining out of your eyes.*
> *Now I'm wise,*
> *And I know what time it is, now.*

Chapter 1

A Touch of the Unthinkable

*B*HAGWAN SHREE RAJNEESH is speaking to five thousand seekers in our meditation hall, high in the Oregon desert. Numb with shock I listen to him reveal that his secretary Sheela has tried to kill his doctor and his personal caregiver.

They'd told me but I hadn't believed them! Cooking for Bhagwan, living in his house—I'm here to wake up, yet I couldn't see a murder plot hatching right under my nose!

Slanting rays of the rising sun stream into the hall, too weak to take the chill off the frosty September morning. Cold from the white linoleum floor seems to creep up my body as Bhagwan continues.

"Vivek got one slow dose of poison, and her heart went absolutely berserk for three hours."

I remember: cooking Bhagwan's supper, the kitchen filled with the sweet/sharp smell of coriander. Vivek coming in with Bhagwan's tray—pale, shaking, unsteady—telling me Sheela had put something in her tea.

Bhagwan goes on. "In the last ceremony Devaraj was injected with poison. He felt the prick, he immediately began saying he had been poisoned. Nobody could believe it."

I hadn't believed it. My mind *wouldn't* believe it. In spite of Devaraj's hammering home the facts, in spite of my own deep distrust of Sheela, in spite of an urgent inner voice that *knew*, I had refused to hear the truth.

Bhagwan's next words rip open the fabric of the Oregon commune. He tells us that Sheela's group had set fire to an office in a nearby town and tried to poison its water supply.

The enormity of it stuns me. Disciples of a master who teaches and lives with total reverence for life—how could they conceive such a scheme? It is more horrendous, more unbelievable than poisoning fellow sannyasins. We have deliberately put ourselves into the hands of a master, knowing full well the risks of playing with the deep unconscious forces of our minds. But these Oregonians are innocent bystanders.

Questions seethe in my mind. *Did Bhagwan know Sheela's potential for violence when he put her in charge of the commune? Did he know of her crimes? If he didn't, why didn't he? If he did, why didn't he stop her?*

In eleven years of living in Bhagwan's commune, nine of those in his own house, nonviolence has become part of my daily life. I capture and set free every fly, bee, wasp and rat that strays inside. On the ranch, deer graze calmly in the open areas around our meditation hall, safe from the guns of Oregon hunters. But now. . . .

How can I explain this cancer of violence at the heart of our peaceful commune?

Bhagwan is speaking, but I am not hearing him; my mind is racing on full throttle. Suddenly I am aware that he has risen and is leaving the hall, hands together in the Indian greeting/farewell called *namaste.*

The hall emptied quickly; everywhere small groups gathered to share their shock. I felt an overwhelming need to be alone.

I stood for long minutes and gazed at our vast meditation hall. The morning sun was striking light from the grooved vinyl roof that dipped and spread out like wings on each side. It looked for all the world like an alien spaceship about to take off. My eyes saw it as if for the first time. *Perhaps the last?* In my heart and guts I knew that our commune, already harassed from all sides because of our different life style, would not survive this calamity.

My feet carried me toward the center of the commune, the city we had built in the past four years. An unpainted barn, relic of the past, looked like an orphan beside all the modern, crisp buildings with their blue/gray wood lapsiding. A long, two story, squarely contemporary building housed the bank and offices. I remembered the time I had phoned my bank in Vancouver to send the total balance, some $50,000, to my account here, and turned it over to the commune. Not a flicker of regret came to me now with the thought.

Next to the bank stood our airport tower, and beyond I could see the runway, looking tiny and fragile in the surround of rocky mountain peaks. I thought of the hangar dismantled, the roar of our planes vanished, weeds pushing through the flawless cement. On the verge of tears, I turned into the shopping plaza. The pizzeria, the ice cream shop, the boutique, the hair salon were buzzing with talk. Only Omar Khayyam, the bar and lounge, stood silent, waiting for the night, when music and laughter would well out into the starlight and the plaza fill with mad dancing. I stood in the silent plaza for long minutes while a sadness beyond tears crept over me.

On the way back to Bhagwan's house, I stopped beside a small creek. The sun was hot but the weeping willows along the creek bed cast a cool shadow. I lay down in a grassy spot to rest, watching muskrats scurry in and out among the bulrushes.

But my mind refused to rest.

How could I, of all people, have been so blind, so unaware of these things happening around me? Years of my life had been spent as a social activist, exposing the blind spots in our social programs: the plight of unmarried mothers, of latchkey children; the poor design and management of public housing. Debating these problems on talk shows put me in the public eye, and led to my being appointed to the board of Canada Mortgage and Housing Corporation, an appointment that required vetting by the federal cabinet.

How could I, dedicated to ferreting out the faults of our western society—how could I not have seen what was going on in Rajneeshpuram? Why had I not spotted the crimes being committed by Sheela and her "moms"?

Racing wildly, my mind slid over my life with Bhagwan, tracing my yoyo plunges from a pompous life style to austere silence and fierce encounters; from the halls of western high finance to the gravel paths of an Indian ashram and the sagebrush hills of an Oregon desert. The kickoff came at a picnic in the park.

Thirteen years ago, as a board member of the powerful Canada Mortgage and Housing Corporation, I had been treated like royalty: the finest hotels and meals, a chauffeur when needed; standing in receiving lines to welcome the financial and political elite of Canada.

I was 48, at the top of my career, when the role of pampered poobah grew stale. So did my role as social activist. A vast discontent seized me. Not how-weary-stale-flat-and-unprofitable discontent, this was champing-at-the-bit discontent. I'd spent a lifetime achieving the goals society sets: satisfying sex, ecstatic love, marriage and children, an honored occupation. All had left me feeling hollow, hungry; wanting, needing something more.

I discovered George Gurdjieff, a twentieth-century mystic whose methods are rooted in the absurd—designed to shock, to rupture the chains of habit, to expose our unconscious actions, to stretch the limits of our normal lives. We acted out roles on the street: a shrew, a pompous ass-hole, a deadbeat; imported a dervish and learned to whirl.

In the summer of 1974 our Gurdjieff group phoned all the religious groups anyone could think of and invited them to a joint potluck picnic in Bear Creek Park outside Vancouver, B.C.

The sun blazed down, children skipped and shouted, swallows swooped and a kingfisher dived in the pool. The eleven groups who came sat at separate tables, making no effort to mingle. The Anglicans brought their knitting and brochures, the Sally Ann, leaflets but not their drums. Scientologists demonstrated the E-meter; two men from The Church of Latter-day Saints talked earnestly and long to the few who stopped by. A bearded man sat in lotus position, silent beneath a sign "TRANSCENDENTAL MEDITATION."

I dropped by at each table, but quickly became dispirited; each one wanted not to converse but to convert. Childhood memories flooded back, a rising tide of anger roiled inside. My father and mother had lived their quiet religion; but my five older sisters joined five different churches, and arguments over the Bible were so ferocious I seldom came into the house.

As I stood reading the tracts handed to me in the park, a vivid scene from the past flashed: *My sister trying to prove that the British, not the Jews, are the lost tribe of Israel. Dad taking the Bible from her, reading out "And Judas went out and hanged himself;" flipping the pages and reading "Go thou and do likewise." Saying "Janet, that's what you're doing—just flipping the pages."*

I looked over the picnic scene in Bear Creek Park, and my anger vanished. My father's insight seemed right on. So many competing messages, so many spiritual paths, each one sure that his was the way! On this glorious sunny day, with the sound of the stream in my ears and the birds singing, I felt sure of one thing: *this is the only church for me.* I relaxed with the kingfishers and the kids.

The quiet of the picnic was shattered by a blast of strident percussion and blaring flute. Everyone goggled at a lean young man in orange with a mass of dark hair falling to his shoulders, gyrating to the music pouring from a tape recorder on the grass. He shook, screamed, sobbed, yelled and danced, his hair swinging wildly, the beads around his neck almost flying off over his head. Twirlingwhirlingleapingswayinglaughing. An atomic explosion in a green desert.

"He's flipped out," I thought to myself. But the music pulled me; it soared and pulsed, my feet twitched and tingled.

I closed my eyes and whirled, and whirled, and whirled. The music crashed to a climax. I fell onto the lush green grass—feeling each blade against my lips, each pounding beat of my heart, each sunray warming my bare legs.

When I opened my eyes the dancer was sitting beside me, smiling. Dangling from a wooden necklace, only inches from my face, swung a locket with a tiny picture inside: a bearded man with twinkling eyes and a mischievous grin.

I stared in wonder, caught in a déjà vu. *I've seen this man before.*

The dancer answered my unspoken questions. "I'm Rammurti," he said, "and that music was a slice of the Dynamic Meditation." He held up the locket. "And this is my master, Bhagwan Shree Rajneesh."

MASTER! I gulped at the word, aghast. This was the first time I'd heard it spoken about someone living. The word gave me a strange feeling, like the shock from a light earthquake.

Two months after the picnic I came across a notice in a community center: "Tonight! The dynamic meditation of Bhagwan Shree Rajneesh!" Something clicked inside.

All day the feeling grew that I had to attend this meditation.

I went out to dinner that night: great food, witty company. But the urge to leave became irresistible. The wide, startled eyes of my hostess as she walked me to the gate burned into my memory. I couldn't explain this sudden departure to myself, how to make sense of it to her? Driving away I found myself laughing out loud, it was so absurd.

By the time I reached the centre the meditation was finished. I felt an odd sense of relief. In one corner an auburn-haired beauty was packing books. She wore a brilliant orange dress with flaring skirt and a fitted bodice that set off her wood bead necklace. We talked as she worked and she grinned infectiously when asked to explain what the meditation was about.

"I honestly don't know if I can," she said. "It's a meditation Bhagwan has created to help throw out the garbage we've got bubbling inside. After it's thrown out, you can move into silence—that's when thoughts stop, when meditation happens. But you really have to try it yourself. Everyone describes it differently."

"What about the necklace, and the orange clothes?" I was determined to get some information now that I was here.

"Bhagwan asks each of us to wear orange and a mala, this necklace," she said, touching it. "I think it's just a sign that we really mean it, that we want to change ourselves enough to risk looking ridiculous. It's part of *sannyas*."

"And what exactly is sannyas?"

The orange dazzler thought for a bit before answering.

"Taking sannyas means that you trust Bhagwan, that you feel he can help you wake up," she said slowly, still packing away the books. "If you go to his ashram in Poona, you can ask for a darshan. That's when you get to see him close up and ask him anything you want.

"If you decide to take sannyas," she chuckled, as if at a private memory, "he gives you a new name to help you drop the past. Traditional sannyasins in India also take a new name and wear orange and a mala. But they renounce the world, and Bhagwan doesn't want us to do that."

I asked if she could recommend a book and she looked down at the small volume in her hands. "This is one I think you'd like, and it's only three dollars," she said, handing it to me.

That night I read *The Silent Explosion* from beginning to end. "The Flight of the Alone to the Alone" proclaimed the first chapter. Those words fell into a place beyond my mind, reverberating like an echo of something already heard. Something inside me jumped for joy, clapped its hands, hugged itself. My heart sang, "This is it! This is the way it is!" A quiet space beyond logic opened up, where the mind couldn't understand, where the mind was not needed at all.

Next morning—with no hesitation, as if everything were happening on its own—I booked a flight to India.

Three months later I was on my way. I took a six-month leave of absence from United Community Services and the board of CMHC, arranged a long-term rental on my house, and said good-bye to my bewildered friends, relatives and three sons. Only my youngest son, Lawrie, was enthusiastic, a little envious even, since it was he who had turned me on to Gurdjieff. My eldest, atheist son Craig was stunned and unhappy. Blair hugged me and joked about gurus. I gratefully accepted a high-necked orange robe sewn for me by a Christian niece.

I don't pretend to explain this irrational leap into the unknown. But then, no one can explain either why homing pigeons "home"; or how the Arctic tern, breaking out of its shell on a tropical island, finds the way unguided to its icy abode thousands of miles away; or why Pacific salmon, after years frisking in the wide ocean, suddenly and surely turn, battering themselves against rocks and whitewater falls to reach their place of origin.

Outside the plane window the sun poured color onto the clouds below. I gazed enchanted, melting into the lacy pink fluff that filled space as far as my eyes could see; feeling the softness of it in my very bones, as if I'd stepped out of the plane and gone rolling in it.

The sun faded soon; I put on a blindfold and my earplugs. As the hours passed I relaxed more and more into the silence. Now I was a solitary planet, flying through darkness; a voyager freed from the bonds of earth, soaring effortlessly through space.

Bursts of energy rushed up my spine, snapped me bolt upright in the seat; hammered inside my forehead, focused between the eyes. I sat unmoving, watching panic, pain, amazement; watching thoughts rush, slow, fade. The hammering died away. Then . . . silence. A silence I had never known, never imagined; cannot convey.

Chapter 2

Meeting with a
Remarkable Man

I LANDED IN BOMBAY on December 18, 1974, in a stifling wave of
humid heat. On the plane, enraptured with silence, I'd decided
not to speak until my meeting with Bhagwan. So I couldn't even
grumble at the heat waving up from the airfield, heavy with moisture
and fumes. No tunnels here to cushion the shock, passengers stepped
off the plane onto sizzling tarmac. The tar burned through the soles
of my shoes, my own sweat dripped into them from above. The air
reeked of gas and oil outside; inside, the building stank of body sweat,
filth and decaying garbage. I'm easy with most smells, but in Bombay
my stomach threatened to offload.

A sea of human flesh engulfed me as I came out of customs. "Taxi?"
"Taxi, baba?" "Taxi!!" Bolder drivers tried to snatch my bags.

"Rupees, mama? Two rupees!" implored hordes of ragged children with big eyes and stick arms. I gave two rupees to one angelic

waif, and the rest closed in. The silence that only minutes before had given wings to my spirit now robbed me of the right to move. Made bold by my silence, the tangle of ragged bodies jostled, clutched, pleaded.

Setting one bag down, I put a finger to my lips, then pointed at myself. As if by magic the hubbub quieted, the wretched sea of humanity opened up—*like the Red Sea*, the thought flashed as I walked through to the exit. I stopped once to shift my suitcases and an old woman darted up to touch my feet. This unseemly respect continued for two years. Every caste in India, from beggar to brahmin, respects one who is *moun*, who has taken a vow of silence.

Blank looks greeted my written queries at "Information" till a richly dressed Indian woman came to my rescue, finding me a taxi, giving the driver directions to the train. When she found my destination was Poona she gave me her card, insisting that I stay in her house as she is a Parsee and most interested in other spiritual seekers. My mind reeling at this overflowing generosity, I nodded and smiled.

It's hard to imagine a more stunning introduction to India than a train journey in the third class compartment I stumbled into. Bodies crowded the aisles, men women children goats chickens, sitting, standing, jabbering. Most men and some women chewed on glossy dark green leaves and every few minutes they shot out streams of bright red juice. They aimed at the sides of the train—there were no spittoons—and everywhere there were long lines of this red spittle, darkening to a blackish brown where it dried. The chewers' gums, lips and any teeth they still possessed were stained dark red; most faces had a sunken, caved-in look. I couldn't believe it was real, so bizarre was that train compartment.

I stared out the window for relief, but there was none—only an endless line of cardboard/mud/tin hovels. At every station beggar women came up to the windows. They looked like birds of prey, all bones and skin and huge eyes that seemed to be devouring me; always they brought children, one clinging to the mother's dirty ragged sari, another on the hip, another on the way. A claw reached through the bars—*"Baksheesh, baba, baksheesh."* From behind the barred windows I passed out rupees, tears rolling down. I'd seen the face of poverty in the West; this was the bare retching guts of it.

Skinny men got on at the stations, walked through with trays of stuffed pastries. With their white clothes and stick legs they reminded me of pelicans. I couldn't eat.

The hideous sprawl of Bombay fell behind and slowly the view framed by the window changed. The shacks, still sketchy but now set among rolling green fields, streams and low hills, looked less wretched.

At one station stop I watched, fascinated, as a group of women walked back and forth, back and forth beside the train. They struck me as royal figures from a distant time, with their erect carriage and graceful movement, swirling saris in flamboyant colors and patterns, arms glistening with bright glass bangles. In their nostrils and ears they wore ornate silver filigree ornaments. Delicate silver jewelry sparkled in their black hair. They laughed and chattered as they walked.

I stared at them in amazement. On her besilvered head, cushioned with a small round cloth, each one carried a pan shaped like a wok, filled with cement or gravel. Dressed in their finery they were working, repairing the road! Some carried a child in a sling on their hip while they worked. Dozens of children with huge sparkling eyes played happily in the sand—the girls like little elves, their hair pulled up in pigtails on top of their heads and tied with ribbons, their ears flaunting tiny earrings. This startling mixture of art and heavy labor, of grace and merriment lighting up a menial chore—mothers surrounded by their children, enjoying—this was the first bit of beauty I'd seen in India.

The train groaned into the Poona station five hours after leaving Bombay, a distance of only a hundred miles. Within seconds a skinny taxi driver swept up my two heavy suitcases and popped them into his battered black Ford. He spoke no English and I was at a loss how to give him directions, till on sudden inspiration I opened a suitcase and pulled out my new orange robe. He beamed. *"Ashram, baba, ashram!"* and we were away.

The December sun touched the tops of huge broadleafed evergreens as the taxi sped through the wide, quiet streets of Poona's Koregaon Park, huge red brick mansions set back on either side. The mansion grounds were deserted except for an occasional servant sweeping the winding drives, tending the majestic gardens. My journey had ended in the last bastion of the old British Raj.

The driver let me out in front of the Shree Rajneesh ashram.

Towering, majestic gates glowed in the afternoon sun. Formed from thick slabs of rosewood, carved with intricate, voluptuous scrolls, studded with huge shiny brass nails and fastened with great brass hinges—these were gates to conjure by. I stood still for a long minute, for all the world like Dorothy standing before the Emerald Gates in the City of Oz, with one difference: these gates were open.

A blonde orange-robed "guard" beckoned me in. He didn't look like a real guard to me, he was dressed in an orange robe, sitting down, with no sign of any weapon. He responded to my note ("Darshan?") by grinning and pointing me down the only path: "Talk to Laxmi in the office. You can leave your suitcases here if you like."

The City of Oz hasn't been built yet, I mused as I walked down the gravel path that led through a weedy garden to a huge, rough concrete building, the only one in sight. On the right stretched a gray canvas tent, undistinguished except for its size; it must have been fifty feet across. I walked past it, up the steps of the grey building, and turned left into a room labeled "office."

Behind an enormous desk sat the tiniest Indian woman I was ever to meet. Her feet didn't reach within six inches of the floor; she perched, like a sparrow about to take flight, on the edge of an enormous chair. Huge brown eyes flashed in a heart-shaped face; a no-nonsense white cap held back a reckless profusion of dark waist-length hair. A small sign on the desk read: Ma Laxmi.

"Can Laxmi help you?" she asked, in excellent English. I looked around; there was no one else in the office. I would soon learn that Laxmi always spoke of herself in the third person, and of Bhagwan in capital letters.

I picked up a pencil and paper from her desk and dashed off a quick note: *Just arrived, want to take sannyas tonight, and to ask Bhagwan whether to remain in silence.*

The pixie brow wrinkled. "You have attended any meditations?"

Dynamic, in Vancouver—a slight exaggeration. But a strange sense of urgency possessed me: I *must* go to darshan, tonight! I remained standing, looking into her eyes, and Laxmi's face relaxed.

"Do you have an orange robe?"

Yes!

"You must pass the sniffers."

A blank look must have crossed my face.

"Bhagwan's body is fragile, smells create for him a problem; you must use shampoo with no scent." Seeing that I was still puzzled, Laxmi picked up a pen and wrote.

"Laxmi will write you the name of a shop. The guard will call you a rickshaw."

She handed me the slip. "You must be at Lao Tzu gate much before seven." She looked at her watch and added, "There is no time today. Laxmi will give you shampoo." She opened a drawer and handed me a small bottle. My face must have shown my gratitude because she smiled, a warm smile that lit up her face as she added, "You are in silence, but still you must speak to Bhagwan in darshan. And His discourse is in the mornings, eight o'clock."

The gate guard beckoned a rickshaw driver and I handed him the Parsee's card. Within two hours I was back in the ashram, bathed, shampooed and dressed in my new orange robe, with half an hour to spare.

I waited with ten others outside the wrought iron gate of Lao Tzu House, the big ancient dwelling in the ashram where Bhagwan lived. Thick red ivy covered the walls of the old mansion, and the wide path was bordered with unknown tropical trees, many in flower; wisps of evening mist clung to their branches. A sense of the sacred came to me. *Mt. Olympus. Home of the gods.*

Going through the orange-clad "sniffers" felt distinctly odd. Two of them, one on each side, stood just inside the gates. They could have been models for any fashion magazine. They were earnest in their job, determined to find any scent that would affect Bhagwan's health. We had to bow our necks as we passed between them, and the thought flashed: *perhaps this ceremony is a symbol of surrender?*

We walked along the gravel path and into the house, then through hushed corridors with high, high ceilings. So deep was the silence any word would have profaned it. Our bare feet made no sound on the polished granite of the floor. The feel of that stone is printed in my memory cells: infinitely smooth, cool, soft.

Suddenly we came onto a large balcony. It seemed to float on a sea of greenery. Huge trees from the garden—some with delicate, feathery foliage, others with broad, round glossy leaves—sent their branches into the space, giving it the feel of a clearing in a tropical jungle. A thousand tiny frog voices and the rustle of birds only deepened the silence.

Bhagwan Shree Rajneesh is already seated in a straight-backed arm-chair. He wears a simple high-necked white robe, so white it appears almost luminous, setting off the black hair falling over his shoulders, the black beard cascading down his chest. We settle in a semicircle on the floor in front of him. Laxmi beckons to me and I find myself sitting at his feet, almost touching him.

He sits, so still, one leg crossed over the other. His hands, with long tapering fingers and fingernails, lie folded, unmoving, in his lap. His stillness reaches out to me, touches me. The silence of those magic moments on the plane wells up inside—the silence of the vast wild spaces of my childhood.

He looks at me, his eyes large, almost black, deep. He looks at me, *looks into me*; I feel known. A flood of well-being courses through my veins, filling dry, parched, unknown corners; a flood of content. Not a high-flying ecstasy, just a simple content, a relaxing: I've come home. Tears roll down, wetting my new orange robe.

He writes slowly, deliberately, on a sheet of creamy paper. Laxmi hands him a mala. He holds it for a moment, then drops it around my neck; the locket crashes on my heart. Solid, tangible, the mala a link, a rope. I am roped to a guide I trust with all my heart and soul. For no reason at all.

He hands me the sheet of paper.

"This will be your new name, Ma Anand Nirgun," he tells me; his voice is very soft. "*Anand* means bliss. But forget the Anand, just remember the *Nirgun*. Nirgun means 'without form.' This whole world comes from the formless. The original source is formless and millions of forms arise out of it.

"All that can be comprehended with the senses are forms arising from the formless. The original source is formless—that which is unseen, unknown. And it is unknowable. You have to drop everything, become absolutely empty; only then you come to know it."

The formless! As I stare at him, images flash somewhere inside; buried memories from the past, glimpses of being formless, outside my body, released now in a strange montage. . . .

I am a small child. The frogpond is deep. My not-much-older brother has chipped a boat out of a log, lifted me into it, pushed it out. I see him crouching on the bank, see his grinning purple face,

Nirupa in darshan with Bhagwan.

the green frogs on the waterlily pads. As if from above I see the frilly white dress I am wearing, the tiny child-body sitting ever so still in the crude boat. Knowing the danger.

Age eight, alone in the woodshed. The washing machine falters. I pour gas into the carburetor as I've seen my father do. The engine backfires with a great roar and a sheet of gas-filled flame shoots up in my face. Suddenly I am separate from the child-body running for the house; below me I see her hair streaming out in flames behind, hear the fire crackling, hear her voice yelling "Help!" Feeling no fear, only a strange freedom.

Age twenty-six, lying on the floor breathing deep, deeper, lungs on fire; preparing for natural childbirth. Suddenly I'm on the ceiling looking down at a shapeless mass in a green maternity suit. In the same instant I am back inside the swollen green form.

Age forty-seven, disenchanted with my life, dabbling in the world of drugs.

Stoned on pot, hearing Mendelssohn's violin concerto
for the first time, again.
High on Orange Sunshine, once and only,
seeing the blue of the sky for the first time

the plumpness of the fuschia in the garden
tasting the purple of pruneplums
. . . seeing into my face in the mirror as
the flesh twitches off in tiny bits
a flick off the corner of the mouth
off the chin off the forehead
the cheek
an infinity of flicks till light years later
  the glowing white skull is exposed
coursing tears (I am not crying)
disappearing
the mirror blank

knowing with a certainty never shaken
this clarity this brilliance this nothingness
this is the way the world is.

I come back to the still room in the Indian night, every sense
alert: To the swelling chorus of frog voices, to the wind rustling the
feathery leaves, to the sharp whiteness of Bhagwan's robe. To the laughing faces of those around me.

Bhagwan sits back in his chair, chuckling.

"Now you will celebrate this day as your birthday," he tells me.
"Body birthdays are really deathdays. People celebrate them to cover
up, to help them forget that one more year has gone by and nothing
has happened to them yet."

His words strike a chord, a simple truth always felt but never
acknowledged. Now I understand why I've never celebrated my birthdays.

Laxmi reminds me of my question. I ask Bhagwan, "Is it good for
me to remain in silence?"

He doesn't answer, just looks into my eyes. I add, "It started on
the plane, and it feels good to continue."

He ponders for what seems eternity, looking down at his hands,
now unfolded, open in his lap. "It is unusual," he says finally. "But if
it feels right to you, there is no harm in it. Not for a set time, just as
long as it feels good. And you will come to darshan and talk to me
every week, h'mmm?"

I float back to my place on the floor, unaware of what a special privilege has been given me.

Others come to sit in front of him, to take sannyas or to ask advice. I hear and see little.

Deep in my belly waves of merriment swell, swell higher; by sheer will I keep them in. Finally Bhagwan stands, slowly, giving total attention to every movement; saluting us with palms together in the Indian greeting/farewell called *namaste*. We respond in kind; my head seems to bow on its own. Then he walks to the door with small, careful steps, as if he is balancing on a tightrope.

My shoulders shake with laughter as I watch him move away. My master! What a hoot, what a hilarity! My eyes follow him till he disappears. Then I melt onto the cool stone floor, a puddle of absurd merriment.

The next day I tore up my return ticket to Canada.

Chapter 3

Let Go!

S IX A.M. The driving beat of heavy drums and tablas shattered the morning stillness of Poona. The big gray canvas tent flamed into motion. Hundreds of orange bodies around me convulsed in a riot of deep fast breathing with the noise of a steam engine roaring to life.

This was Dynamic Meditation, Bhagwan's technique to throw our garbage out and make room for something new.

The leader's voice shocked me wide awake. "*Breathe!* Deeper, faster empty your lungs!" Hands on my knees, I pressed down, forcing the air out, sucking it in, my body a giant bellows. "Breathe *deep*—stake everything!" My lungs breathed fire. A great energy charged the air of the tent.

The music changed. "Let go of your body now . . . let it move as it will, let it cry or dance, leave it free."

The tent filled with screams, shouts, sobs; bodies fell, writhed, pounded. "Let go! Let your whole being shake if it wants. Let go of the body." I rolled on the floor, laughing, crying.

A "let-go" meditation in Buddha Hall.

The music moved to a heavy, steady percussion. "Jump and shout Hoo! Hoo! Hoo!"

All around me bodies surged into the air, "Arms up, higher, higher, land on your *heels*!" Arrows of pain shot up my legs; they could not, would not lift the heavy stone of my body.

"Total, be total!" He was talking to me, I knew it. My body jumped higher.

"Stop!" Abrupt silence. My arms froze above my head. The sudden stop sent energy hurtling through me. I felt the thrust of it pulling in my gut, rampaging up my spine, centering between the eyes; blacking out all thought, all feeling, leaving only a deep silence.

A distant flute piped, light, joyful. The strains of a sitar joined in. Every pore of my body opened, every body fiber drank in the melody and joined in the dance, dipping, swaying, whirling on its own.

The music faded. We stretched out, face down on the hard ground. Lying there, bodies close together, I felt a strange intimacy with these total strangers, as if we shared some precious secret.

After dynamic the smell of coffee and new-baked bread drew me to a tiny canteen, to a breakfast of bruns and curd, bananas and papayas.

I ate sitting on the ground with a few dozen sannyasins who overflowed the tiny space, watching them in total amazement. They were characters out of a medieval novel. The women had shining, beautiful hair, shoulder length or longer. Although they all wore orange and a mala, the effect was not of a uniform; colors ranged from saffron to rust, styles from demure to provocative. Most wore long loose robes of cotton, but some were gauzy, see-through; the effect was aesthetic and sensual. The men had long hair too and dressed in loose orange robes; many had beards. Men and women both seemed to float rather than walk.

Suddenly I saw that I too was wearing an orange robe! not the black latex pants and dark shirt I'd worn on the plane. Overnight I had dropped out of the era of black-and-white movies into the glories of technicolor. My past life began to fade, withdraw, as if it had also belonged to some far distant era.

Someone looked at a watch and the crowd began drifting down the path toward Lao Tzu House. Passing through the sniffers at the gate, we followed the path beside the house; it led into a large open-sided auditorium, set in a lush garden.

Promptly at eight Bhagwan came onto the podium, namasted in his slow, careful way, sat down and began to speak.

I hadn't brought a cushion, and the chipped marble floor was hard. The hall was full of immense, hungry mosquitoes. It was cold, really cold, and I hadn't brought a sweater. I wanted Bhagwan to talk about Dynamic Meditation, explain what it was all about, but he didn't. Complaint after complaint grouched inside.

But somewhere in the next two hours my complaining mind took a holiday. I became aware of his presence in the chair and the gestures of eloquent hands as he poured out what seemed to me the wisest, most entertaining talk I had ever heard.

After the discourse I borrowed a book from the office and read Bhagwan's brief comments on the morning meditation.

"When you are doing the Dynamic, this is not really meditation. First you have to throw out all the junk, speediness, impatience, hurry, repressions that prevent you from going into silence. You have woken yourself up by jumping, dancing, breathing, shouting. These are all devices to make you more alert. Then—waiting. *Waiting with full awareness is meditation.*"

Waiting for what? For the inner silence when thoughts stop.

Each of Bhagwan's meditations led to this silence in a different way: *Nadabrahma* through humming, *Nataraj* through dancing, *Kundalini* through shaking, *Vipassana* through simply watching the breath. For four months I did all five every day.

But after each meditation the inner quiet gave way to thoughts, the mind sprang back to life. Desire replaced delight. I wanted in. I craved enlightenment with the fierce self-will of Captain Ahab in pursuit of the white whale. The path of aloneness lay clear ahead; my silence stood guard against intruders.

I read of a meditation camp near Lonavala, twenty miles away, where any seeker could stay for three weeks in a rough cabin, seeing no one; food and boiled water would be brought nightly by the camp manager for a small charge.

"Should I go?" I ask Bhagwan in my weekly darshan. "If I go, should I stay inside the whole time or is it okay to take walks?"

"It is fine for you to go," Bhagwan replies. He massages my third eye; I see a flash of light, so like a photographic flash I look around for the camera. I know how tricky the mind can be, and am British-suspicious of uncanny experiences. But this flash is sudden, unexpected, with no time for the mind to come in.

Bhagwan smiles. "Nirgun, you have a *very active* mind," he tells me, in a serious tone that belies the smile. "It will go off in fantasies if you even see a dog while you are walking. You will think about every dog you ever knew." *Rover, the love of my childhood, appears to me the same instant: his shiny tan coat and big white ruff, the feel of his soft fine hair under my fingers, his wet nose nuzzling into my palm.*

I come back to the present. Bhagwan has paused and is just looking at me, chuckling. "So it would be better not to go out of the cabin unless you wear a blindfold, h'mmm?" he tells me. "And every day do this one new meditation: just stand in a corner and talk gibberish for half an hour. No words, no language, just nonsense sounds. Will it be alright?"

I nod, swelling with delight at being given something to do, no matter how absurd.

"Come out of silence just for the trip there, just till you are settled. And come to darshan as soon as you get back, h'mmmm? Good, Nirgun."

Lonavala proved to be just an hour down the line. My voice, asking directions at the Poona station, sounded in my ears like the voice of a stranger—for the past four months I had been in silence except for a few moments speaking to Bhagwan in my weekly darshan. The same stranger's voice ordered tea and samosas on the way, then asked how to get to the cabins, a mile out of town. There I found the caretaker, an old man who spoke no English but managed to convey that he didn't cook meals, he would leave water and fruit.

The tiny cabin was glutted with furniture: a cot, a table and seven chairs. I piled them in the centre of the room, ran and walked around them for exercise; spouted gibberish for half an hour each day, plunged into all the ashram meditations; sunbathed outside with a blindfold, put a pebble on the window sill each time to mark another day. For hours I watched my breath coming in, going out, coming in, going out. . . .

And slowly the certainty comes to me that I am not breathing, I am being breathed. On the third day a rush of energy hurtles up my spine, hammers on the third eye. Every day the pounding grows stronger. By the eighth day the muscles of my face join in the madness. They stretch and contract in hideous grins and grimaces. Day after day the spasms come—faster, more powerful, more painful. My jaw stretches: to the right, to the left, now up, now down. The masks I've worn throughout my life are crumbling, my face is doing all the things it always wanted to do.

Time vanishes—a week, two weeks, two and a half. The painful stretching dies away. I am alone, resting in a quiet space. Thoughts too seem to have faded, to exist only on the edges of a vast inner silence. Three weeks.

The trail to the Lonavala station was narrow and stony. Prickly bushes grew out from the sides and scratched my legs; I felt it, but not as pain, it was just happening. The low green hills, the twisty gray trees, the brown and green fungus on the ponds blended together in a rich tapestry of color and form. I must have been wearing blinkers when I came, not to have noticed the newness, the freshness all around.

In the village my feet pulled me to the side of the road where a very old tiny Indian tended a barber's chair. I sat in it and signalled him to shave off my hair. He asked no questions, simply shaved it off;

I gave him all the rupees I had. My body floated on its way, my whole being filled with the absurd delight of an infant discovering its toes.

But even while the train clacked and rumbled its way back to Poona, the old mind began to clack and rumble too. Calculating the odds on enlightenment happening in this lifetime, greedy to hold onto this moment.

Bhagwan often joked about enlightenment, telling us we are already enlightened, we just have to dig away the pile of rubbish accumulated since birth.

"You are ninety-nine percent unconscious," he told us solemnly one day, "and that one percent I leave you just not to shock you too much."

Freud gave us ten percent, not one, I thought glumly, still gazing out the window. Now that my frenetic mind had kicked in I barely noticed the green valleys and bare hills. The impatient quest was on again, the starter's flag had dropped, cutting off the reality of here and now. My mind bubbled with thoughts of a further and higher destination. Hellbent for enlightenment.

In darshan that night I sit in front of Bhagwan and he looks at me with his bottomless eyes. He chuckles and says, "How are you, Nirgun?"

"Just great, Bhagwan," I tell him. And I am. Here in front of him an easy contentment settles on me as gently as a duvet settling on my body at night.

Thoughts cut off. I'd intended to tell him everything, even rehearsed it. But I just sit, grinning like a baboon, without a care or a thought in the world.

"Any questions?" Bhagwan asks, and my head shakes: no. He tells me to close my eyes and touches my third eye. Then he chuckles again and says, "Very good, Nirgun."

But now Dynamic didn't fit with me any more. Only with gigantic effort did I crawl out of bed each morning, trudge an endless mile to the ashram and manage a lukewarm catharsis. I told myself not to drag my heels, redoubled my efforts. Weeks crawled by. Vipassana and Nadabrahma began to lose their magic. Five months, six. . . .

Westerners were pouring into the ashram, many staying indefinitely, lodging in the City of Poona or in makeshift huts by the river.

In the ashram rooms were added onto existing buildings to house the growing number of workers: therapists, construction workers, maintenance and cooking staff, doctors and nurses.

Meditations were free. They moved from the tent to a big open-sided hall with a floor of chipped marble, directly behind the offices. A new restaurant with a varied menu opened on the other side.

During his years of touring the country, speaking to large crowds, Bhagwan had attracted thousands of Indian disciples. They swarmed into the ashram for their five annual religious holidays. The ashram turned itself into a Mardi Gras each time: every pathway, every building flaunted gay banners and lights; dancing, singing, feasting filled the spaces between discourse, darshan and meditations.

Despite the gaiety of the ashram, my strange mood, my dwindling interest in meditations, persisted.

Why didn't I ask Bhagwan for guidance? I could speak to him in darshan even though I was in silence the rest of the time. Later he told us that meditations are not to be chosen for a lifetime, that the needs of each seeker change along the way.

But the ego cannot admit failure, cannot ask for help. I had set a course to enlightenment and I blundered on with my five-meditations-per-day routine. The craving was still there, stronger than ever, to peek in at *myself*, at the stranger within the gate. But the gate was locked, the path had vanished. Seven, months, eight, nine. . . .

One night in darshan Bhagwan told me to drop *all* meditations. He looked around at the others in the room and added, sternly, "I am telling this just to Nirgun." No hint of a reason—and I didn't ask, just let delight wash over me. *I* knew it was right, but how did *he* know? He was speaking with my own inner voice. I could have listened to myself months before—to the sound of my feet dragging, to the feel of my spirits slumping. The message from me and from Bhagwan was one and the same: time to relax, let go. Let go of effort.

Monsoon season was upon us. Rains that had been a nuisance now poured on me in exuberant baptism. Each afternoon the sky ripped open and RAIN took over the world. Warm rain, great spouts of it. I ran down the stairs and threw myself into it, delighting; ran the full mile to the ashram. My wet robe clung to my skin, water poured down my back. Shocks of warm wind whipped across my face, tore flowers and branches from the trees. In minutes the road turned into a foot-deep torrent where banana fronds and hibiscus and jacaranda blossoms jockeyed for partners in a redgreenpurple dance of abandon. I danced with them, ecstatic, face-up to the flood, tongue thrust out to taste the rain. Remembering. . . .

It was raining, a cold hard rain. I was eleven. When I came out of school the river was swelling over its banks. The churning water picked up the silt from the bottom and turned the river into a spring freshet, a yellow torrent capped with foam.

I stepped into my canoe and shoved off, into the mouth of a roaring cannon. The plunging water tore deadheads and snags loose from the bank, hurled them down like missiles, invisible in the snarling yellow flux till only a paddle length away. The fierce current made steering impossible. I could only meet each danger as it came, twisting parallel with a savage backstroke.

I reached our side of the river a mile downstream; drenched, ecstatic.

My childhood home was in Kingcome Inlet, 250 miles north of Vancouver on Canada's wild west coast. Across the river was another pioneer family, and the schoolhouse; a mile upriver, a Native Indian reservation. That was it.

The mountains in Kingcome Inlet plunged straight into the sea; the word "road" wasn't in our vocabulary. It took four hours by gasboat to the nearest floathouse community with a tiny store, eight hours to the nearest doctor. We had no electricity but we did have plenty of running water; it poured out of the sky, 144 inches per year.

Kingcome River flowed just a hundred feet from our door. She ran full in summer but in winter wandered in and out of silver sandbars, lean and lackadaisical, resting in pools of colored pebbles.

Her magic flowed through my early life. At ten I made a hideaway in a great cedar grove near the water's edge, more than a mile from our house. Mossy logs for sitting, a soft floor of moss for lying. I plaited the low scented boughs together, making a cover to keep out all but the fiercest rain, leaving a tiny glade open to the sun and moon.

Every Sunday I paddled and poled the mile upstream to deliver our tithe of vegetables and milk to the Anglican mission on the reservation. The sermons left me cold, but the Kwakiutl music enchanted:

Nirgun at 18 months (far right) with her family in British Columbia.

the strange harmonies, the heavy rhythmic beat solid as the earth under my bare feet, flowing as the river.

When the sun shone I'd slide on past the farm, slowly, the paddle finding that same rhythmic beat, on to where the river flowed into the ocean. I'd sit with small waves rocking the canoe and stare at the rich green mountains in their endless plunge into the blue-green sea; gaze at the redrock face that had once been a huge slide scar, now mellowed into a fantasy of color and form with huckleberry and green alder and moss, the white tracery of waterfall cutting through it as if painted with one stroke of an artist's brush. A deep hush, a magic silence, an ecstasy . . . knowing that I am part of this, that there is no place where it begins and I leave off. The vast mysterious beauty of Kingcome reached to my inner core and dropped anchor there.

Now the same ecstasy fills me as I dance in the monsoon rains on the other side of the world. And in morning discourse with Bhagwan the same mysterious beauty engulfs me. When he enters everything seems to part and make way for him, then fold itself around him. He turns slowly, palms together, to greet us, seeming to seek out the face of each one. Warm blood courses through my arms, hands, face. As he steps carefully to the podium I steal a glance around me. Every face is lit with joy as if a lamp had been switched on inside. I know mine is alive with the same glow.

He sits in his chair, slips one foot out of its thong and crosses his left knee over the right. Just so will he sit on many different stages, to begin each of the thousands of talks I will hear over the next sixteen years. Relaxed, totally still.

Only his hands move, infinitely graceful hands, to reinforce his points. To bring alive the message of "enlightened ones," human beings who have brought their consciousness to a full flowering: Christ, Lao Tzu, Socrates, Zarathustra, Heraclitus, Pythagorus, Sufi masters, Zen masters.

On this day Bhagwan is speaking on Buddha, in English with a strong Indian accent; without notes, without hesitation—his voice soft and sibilant, the s's drawn out.

As he gestures with his long fingers, two tiny brown birds are dancing, courting in the air above his head. Suddenly the female drops down and clings to one finger—just clings there, for what seems an eternity. Bhagwan's hand has stopped at the touch. It remains upraised, motionless as he speaks on, missing never a word. The bird flies away. My breath rushes out, my heart floods with wonder.

Chapter 4

Rebellions Revisited

*S*TOPPING ALL MEDITATIONS left a great gap in my life—for one day. With a magic slate from a local store (messages could be written and zipped off) I flashed a quick query "Need Help?" to Mukta, the head gardener. It brought a grin to her expressive mouth; her big brown eyes danced and she gave me a great hug.

Member of a wealthy Greek shipping family, Mukta had been with Bhagwan since the beginning of sannyas. "Do your own thing" seemed to be her leit motif; she turned me loose in the sprawling gardens with only one instruction, "Don't prune anything!" So for weeks I weeded and hoed, hoed and weeded; it wasn't the season for planting, and the monsoons took care of watering.

One morning after breakfast my stomach rebelled at the smell of shit coming from the five Indian toilets grouped close to the meditation hall. They were tiny rough shacks with a gross stained hole in the concrete floor to crouch over, shit and urine spattered on walls and floor—gut wrenching, awful. Sannyasins lined up at the toilets after discourse, after meals, after meditations, and no one seemed to clean the shacks, ever. The caste system forbade any Indian but a sudra (the lowest caste) to touch excrement. And Westerners, including me, had been taught from birth that shit is nasty. So no one volunteered.

The job had to be done, and there was no one to do it. Without asking I took cleaning supplies from the open cupboards in the hallways. Because the toilets were in constant demand, to close even one proved impossible; people pounded on the door. To clean them I stood in line with the stream of defecators and urinators. Bright orange robe tucked into huge rubber boots, wearing a thick gauze mask, cleaning tools clutched in both gloved hands, I'd enter the horror shack. But no gauze could keep out the hideous stench. Stomach churning, throat gagging, I'd scrub and slosh till the knocking on the door became frantic, then come out to join the line again; wait; enter, scrub and slosh, leap out. . . .

The toilet fandango became a powerful meditation. Because the job was so loathsome, so disgusting, I had to separate myself from it, become totally detached. This happened by itself; I began to watch "my" disgust and loathing from a distance, not seeing it as mine.

Finishing each toilet I painted the interior of each shack with daffodil-yellow calcomine, bought for a pittance at the store down the road. The effect was electric. Gratitude showered on me in beaming smiles, nodding heads, namastes. I smiled back, watching my warm feelings with the same detachment. For the first time I experienced my self as separate from my feelings; they were there, but "I" wasn't affected by them.

Checking for mail in the outer office a few weeks later, I found a note asking me to see Laxmi. She had never asked to see me before, and uneasiness gripped me. I knew now that she lived in Lao Tzu, that she saw Bhagwan daily and took direction from him. Her tiny figure, perched on the edge of the huge chair, looked bigger now. She spoke without preamble.

"Nirgun, you are invited to move in the ashram."

Move into the ashram! I knew this invitation was seen as a gift by sannyasins: a symbol of coming closer to the master, a sign of spiritual growth. But the skin on the back of my neck tightened, the hairs rose.

My hands clenched and unclenched, pulled the magic slate from my pocket and wrote, "What would be expected of me?"

"Laxmi thinks it would be good if you cared for the new house and gardens we have purchased next door. It is empty now, you may move in. We ask five thousand dollars."

"I don't have any money." I scribbled, fast, relief flooding.

"Laxmi asks everyone to try to find the money." Her voice remained calm, untroubled. "It is how we manage the ashram. But you can move in now and bring Laxmi the money when you can."

She smiled an end to the interview, then added as I stood up, "Perhaps you will wish to view it from the road. Bhagwan has named it Jesus House. It is needed to turn left from the back gate."

I walked slowly down the gravel path past the office, past Lao Tzu house, heading for the back gate, my mind chattering furiously. Why should I move? I had hated staying with the Parsee; she owned 1000 saris and a home so choked with rare furniture I felt choked as well . . . I loved my two-bedroom apartment on Boat Club Road, just a mile from the ashram, with a monthly rental of only $125 I lived high off the hog on the $600 rent from my Vancouver home . . . How could I give up my private refuge, its airy space, its cool majestic marble counters? . . . Could I live in the busy ashram and remain in silence? . . . I'm a loner at heart, I will not jump with barbarous multitudes.

A lump came in my throat, tears brimmed in my eyes. What would it be like to live in the ashram? . . . Was anyone else in silence? . . . And even if there was, we couldn't communicate . . . The wild babble of the mind went on and on.

I turned left at the back gate and walked fifty feet to the house adjoining the ashram. Then I leaned over the fence, and stared. Jesus House rose like a small, weathered castle. Ancient white plaster, crumbling in places, a turret in the center with rows and rows of windows, rounded wings on each side. The garden—where was the garden? Such a mansion cried out for beds of bloom. The dead remains of flowers showed in big clay pots on the verandas; just inside the fence I saw a long narrow bed of fading calla lilies. They weren't fading naturally. The monsoons were over; they were dying of thirst.

In that second it became clear to me that I would move into the ashram. I saw that my urge to explore, to grow, had slipped into its polar opposite: security at any price, the need to control my life.

Thus spake the rational mind, but after the fact. In truth, I joined the ashram in answer to the cry of a thirsty calla lily.

After discourse the next day I ran to Jesus House. As the first and only resident I chose a large room, writing a note to Laxmi that one or more of my sons would come to visit—though not one had even hinted at it—and I would need space for them. Laxmi sent word that the room was to be renovated for a couple; I was to take the tiny turret room.

A flurry of rebellious thoughts rocked me. It made sense, of course. I'd paid no money to the ashram, and anyway why should a single person occupy one of the large choice rooms? But the thought of my sons coming, feeling unwelcome, made me furious. I sat and watched anger bubble up, burst in sparks over the head of tiny Laxmi. Then sadness washed away the anger: I missed my kids.

Dreaming of the future, yearning for the past, I found myself drifting far from the present, in spite of knowing that existence has only one time: Now.

I moved into the turret room the same hour, a space only seven by eight feet but opening out on fifty feet of roof terrace. Tiny pieces of white tile set at a slight angle made the surface of the terrace seem liquid, as if the sun and moon were shining on the ocean—a sparkling private paradise.

From dawn to dusk the garden absorbed my full energy. The earth everywhere was baked, caked hardpan. Akbar, an Indian mali, was sent to help me. Together we dug a trench three feet deep and three feet wide around Jesus House. For days donkeys decorated with tiny bells tinkled through the gate, bringing in 78 cartloads of manure. I ordered it and paid for it myself, and for all other garden needs. It seemed a small contribution; no one then or ever brought up the question of payment for my room.

As the trench gaped and was filled we coaxed each drooping shrub out of its pot, patted it into the deep rich soil.

Four days into the planting project, my homespun robe sticky with sweat and dirt, I looked up to see Mukta—and Bhagwan! in his immaculate white robe and sandals! standing on the lawn not more than six feet away.

The shock brings blood rushing to my cheeks. He never comes out of Lao Tzu House, never wanders around like this—and I'm really *filthy.*

My grubby hands fly together, returning his namaste.

"How are you, Nirgun?" he asks. His voice amazes me, so soft in the open without a microphone. And he's so small, only a couple of inches taller than me, and I'm 5'3". Close up, his eyes are even larger, darker.

Finally I manage, "I'm just fine, Bhagwan."

He turns to Mukta. "Keep the lawns," he says, "and the trees. Flowers are also good, and many more trees. Nirgun will look after the garden." He looks at me, smiling. "It is okay, Nirgun?"

I look into his bottomless eyes, now so close to mine. My head nods, keeps nodding, idiotically. He is chuckling as he namastes in farewell.

Giving me the garden proved a great gift—the greatest. I popped seeds into the rich soil and brilliant magenta morning glory shot thirty feet to the roof of Jesus House in weeks. Dozens of feathery trees, flaming hibiscus, giant elephant ears—tropical plants galore filled in the spaces and grew inches each day. Once a bamboo stake being used to support a young tree took on a new life of its own, shooting out great spikes that uncurled into a shower of green leaves. The sun rose and shone in a cloudless sky. I lived in a storm of delight, flying weight-less down the long stairs each morning, filled with the exuberance I had felt as a child. . . .

Outside chores rescued me from the clatter and tangle of our ten-child family. In an open shelter I churned the big fat barrel of cream till the butter clotted together, then put the whey in a slop pan for the chickens. Washed and washed the clots in big tubs until the water ran away clear, then kneaded the bright yellow butter with a long paddle on a shiny cedar table. Squeezed out the water till not a drop was left, then pressed the gooey mess into a wooden mold. Hey presto! Out came an exact pound of butter. It was magic, and I was the magician. I wrapped each pound gently and stored it in the glacial river.

In spring a thin smelt-like fish, the oolichan, swarmed up Kingcome River, turning it black. I paddled out into the roiling mass and dipped them in over the side with a handnet. They were so thick that trying to escape some collided and flipped over the side into the boat. As the bubbling mass filled the canoe I felt a warm rush of gratitude: that we could be fed so easily, so certainly, so abundantly.

The same well-being swept over me some mornings watching the warm milk steam as it jetted into the cold pail; seeing the cows kick up their heels when I chased them out to pasture at dusk, listening to their bells fade away; munching sweet whitney crabs in the hayloft and smelling the honey of timothy and clover, the moon a mysterious globe framed in the big barn window.

Working in the garden of Jesus House, I felt the same sense of abundance and gratitude. But after only two weeks Laxmi destroyed my blissful state. She found me in the garden and with no warm-up said, "Nirgun, it is needed that you keep the stairs and hallways of Jesus House clean."

Her words sent shockwaves all the way to my toes. Doesn't she know I'm working more than twelve hours a day? I ran for my magic slate and wrote feverishly, trying to keep up to my feverish thoughts. Notes about the garden . . . impossible to do more. Laxmi said little, just shook her head gently, repeating "It is needed."

She started back up the road to the main ashram. I ran beside her, a thing demented—hands shaking, eyes blurring, seeing only that my glorious freedom was being rudely snatched away. And it was my garden, Bhagwan had personally asked me to take care of it . . . scribble, scribble, frantic.

Sannyasins stopped in their work to stare at what must have been a ludicrous sight. I towered over tiny impeccable Laxmi, my shorn hair a flying chaos, rage shooting out through my huge horn-rimmed glasses; hissing like a pressure cooker about to explode.

We reached Lao Tzu gate, beyond which I could not follow her. Laxmi smiled her quiet smile and said, "Nirgun, you might try it for a few days?"

The next morning I flung myself out of bed, filled two pails with hot soapy water, grabbed the mop from the closet and climbed the long winding stairs to the top floor. I'd forgotten the broom. Suddenly rage overwhelmed me. I will not! I heaved the pails of soapy water down the stairwell. Slammed the mop on the bannister, breaking it. Hurled the broken pieces after the pails. Sat down on the top step, and howled.

Howled and cried and screamed like a two-year-old deprived of her lollipop. Letting out all the pent-up rage from a thousand injustices of my growing-up years. Just feeling the torrent of pain, the agony of being young, dependent on others for my very existence—unfree.

My whole body became one great howl of misery. The open stairwell became a vast sounding board. Howls and screams bounced off the walls, off the ceiling, filling the space with their echoes.

Marvellous echoes—all of a sudden I found myself listening to them, amazed at the glory of the sound. I listened till they faded away, vanished. And with them vanished the anger and pain, washed clean away by the torrent.

I sat on in the quiet stairwell, remembering past outbursts of fury.

My menses started at age ten, flooding my body with hormones that could find no outlet. I turned savage. The hair on the back of my neck stood up at the thought of weeding or milking or churning butter. Dishes broke, cows kicked over the pail. I pulled out a hundred hills of squash Dad had planted among the rows of potatoes. He'd told us a weed is any plant that differs from the rest and this was, after all, a row of potatoes. The squash were just coming into flower and I uprooted them with fiendish delight, as if to destroy the troublesome weed that had invaded my body.

Anger flooded over me when I came across my mother in the garden, always on her knees, her whole existence swallowed up in caring for us. Our simple idyllic life had its roots in slavery. I swore to myself I would never, never, not ever be trapped as she is—a slave to nature and to circumstance. Every hour ruled by the demands of others. The hair at the back of my neck rose at the thought.

I couldn't work beside her. I would leave her there, escape into the woods.

Mother asked me to set the table; I was reading a novel, everyone else was busy. After her third request I rose slowly, still reading, and started to set out dishes with one hand. In impotent rage Dad picked up a teaspoon and started beating me on the head with it.

"Lawrie, how could you!" mother gasped.

Father's answer was a shout that still rings in my ears. "There is a point beyond which endurance becometh a crime!"

For years I thought it was a quote from the Bible.

Now I sat on the top step of the wide stairway of Jesus House, looking around the vast hallway as if seeing it for the first time. A light, bright space—the sun blazed through dozens of windows that followed the line of the freestanding stairs and looked out on the new bed of hibiscus. The stairwell rose in great sweeps, outlined with bannisters of rich red teak—a magical winding staircase leading up and up toward the high vault of the roof. Marred only by muddy stair treads and debris scattered by the construction workers.

I ran downstairs for a broom and another mop. Ran with the same lightness of spirit, the same joy I felt when flying to the garden each morning. And soon fell into the old, rhythmic beat. Paddling a canoe. Churning butter. Digging a trench. Mopping a wide, free-floating staircase. In harmony again.

In the lull after the storm, understanding came on its own. Some part of me had long recognized how strong was the "I" "Me" "Mine" of the ego, the overpowering urge to be in control. But never before had I seen so clearly its devastating force.

I'd always gotten my own way by full-out effort. I seem to have been born with a superstrong urge to explore life on my own, not to be influenced by others; to be free come hell or high water. Only following that urge ever led me to moments of magic. But in my ignorance I didn't know that the innocent urge to be, to be free, to follow one's inner star slides unnoticed into the desire to do, to achieve, to control.

I felt grateful for having caught myself in the act, and resolved to stay alert, not get caught in the same old ego trap.

But a short time later the trap snapped shut again. This time it caught me by the other foot: in the role of boss, not servant.

The smouldering fire within me flamed up over smoking. It was permitted in the commune only in designated areas called smoking temples. One moonlit night I swooped down on a group of smokers—scowling, waving my arms like a dingbat, writing notes and brandishing a sign *!!!NO SMOKING IN THE GARDEN!!!* They left reluctantly, laughing when Teertha, leader of the encounter group, snapped to attention and saluted me as "The Commandant of Jesus House Garden."

This prompted me to write to Bhagwan, telling him how I loved working in the garden but hated to be the boss, ordering other people around.

"Can't you give me a job where I can just work in the garden without having to tell others what to do?" my letter inquired, in all humility.

His answer in a discourse to a packed auditorium stung, deep and painful.

"It's certainly difficult to play an authoritative role, Nirgun," he said. "But the difficulty arises not because of the role but because of the unconscious desire to dominate. You can repress the desire, you can avoid any authoritative role; the desire will remain there. Whenever the role is given to you, the desire hidden in the unconscious becomes alive, jumps on the role. Rather than getting rid of the role, it is better to get rid of the desire to be authoritative.

"So, Nirgun, it is good that you are placed in a role where again and again you will have to say to people, 'Don't do this.' I have put many people in authoritative roles; that is the only way to get rid of any repressed desire.

"And Nirgun has that desire, deep down; hence the fear. She would like some work where there is no need to say to people, 'Do this. Don't do this.' Very easy. But how will you get rid of the subtle, aggressive energy in you?

"I would like you to use these situations. Every situation has to be used in such a way that it helps your spiritual growth.

"So, Nirgun, be more conscious, be more loving. Don't allow that urge to dominate to become an unconscious trip, that's all. Become conscious of it. Through consciousness it will be dropped."

Blushing, embarrassed, wounded, ashamed, grateful for the reminder—a chorus of conflicting feelings welled up as I took to heart this gentle public hit.

That night I made some lighthearted no smoking signs. I'd suddenly become aware that new sannyasins couldn't tell that this new garden was part of the ashram. And perhaps the old-time sannyasins were embarrassed by exposure of their secret smoking. The problem died away.

Yet another hit came my way in discourse. Bhagwan was talking about inner and outer silence. "Nirgun has learned outer silence," he said, and my body froze at the mention of my name. "She has come halfway. But inside, the chattering still continues. That too must drop away."

My throat closed, my cheeks flamed: that my horrid secret should be exposed! How did he know? At the same time I listened, every sense alert, for the secret of how to drop the inner chatter.

But that was all he said. My mind went bananas, filled with rebellious thoughts. What could I do about it, for God's sake? My mind had always raced along in overdrive; it had a mind of its own. I could do without talking, that came easy, but how to shut down the mind's chatter was beyond me. Sometimes it stopped on its own—but why? What was the secret?

Finally I gave up and just sat, watching his hands move, his quiet presence in the chair; listening to the merry twittering birds; feeling the tiny breeze on my back. And walking out at the end, became aware that for many minutes the chattering mind had shut down of its own accord.

Chapter 5

Family Shenanigans

$\mathcal{F}$ROM THE WORLD outside the commune came a cyclone that broke open my peaceful cocoon. A year and nine months after I came to the ashram, Lawrie, my youngest son, arrived. As a teenager he'd been interested in spiritual matters; in fact he had introduced me to Gurdjieff. When I sent him a book of Bhagwan's discourses, he decided on the spot to come to the ashram.

Lawrie brought with him his heart companion. I fell in love with Colleen[†] in the Green Hotel that first day. Perhaps just the sight of her, her mass of red-red hair, her flawless white skin—she was a real beauty. But her face was drawn with distress and disgust. The small hot hotel room, windows closed shut with cobwebs, filthy dark blue walls and giant cockroaches, would horrify anyone coming from the West. And Colleen had been trained as a medical assistant, with high, high standards of cleanliness. Her lips were pressed tight and in her chestnut brown eyes I saw fear? anguish? I'd never been close with women, but just seeing her, my heart went out to Colleen.

---

† This name and her sannyasin name have been altered at her request to protect privacy.

The feeling was not mutual. Years later she told me, "You exploded into the room like a human bomb and threw yourself into Lawrie's arms. I sat on the bed watching you and Lawrie laughing and crying and hugging each other, and I felt a great shock of jealousy because Lawrie was so thrilled to see you. We never hugged in our family." (Neither did we! I yearned to yell, but didn't interrupt her.)

"You gave me a bear hug and held me back to look at me. And I felt you liked what you saw because you smiled, a big beaming smile, looking right into my eyes. A message of affection. But I didn't, I *couldn't* respond. You were smaller and rounder and younger than I'd expected, full of bounce. It didn't fit with my idea of older women. I really *hated* you."

But for me, right from that first moment she was the daughter I hadn't even known I wanted. A year later I would take her side in a heartbreaking clash with my beloved son.

We bought simple round-necked robes for them in the new ashram shop and before eight the next morning we presented ourselves for discourse at the entrance to Buddha Hall, our new meditation and discourse hall that had just been completed. A vast building, it could hold up to 10,000. The slightly-peaked roof, a shining expanse of sheet metal, covered the open-sided hall, its oval shape made it inviting.

But we weren't allowed in.

Five days in a row Colleen was "sniffed out": in spite of endless shampooing, scent still lingered in her long thick hair. We all waited, in a fever of expectancy. Finally on the sixth day the sniffers gave us the nod. The hall was crowded, we had to sit near the back. And when Bhagwan came in and started to speak, he spoke in Hindi! He changed, month and month about; I'd forgotten to warn them. To me, understanding the words wasn't important. And after their first startled look, it didn't bother Lawrie or Colleen either.

At the end of discourse we sought out Mukta and booked a darshan—now held in Chuang Tzu—for the evening.

We skip down the winding path to the open-sided auditorium. Chuang Tzu at night is a magic space. The lights are recessed in the bushes and shine on the fluted green and white Grecian pillars. The colored marble floor gleams like a lake in moonlight. Everyone is

Nirgun and Saguna (opposite page) in darshan session at the Poona ashram.

gussied up as if they are going to a dress ball.

Suddenly Bhagwan appears. Beside me Colleen draws a long shivering breath. Lawrie is called up first. He looks stunned when Bhagwan asks if he wants to take sannyas. He sits there bewildered, rubbing his chest, and finally blurts out, "Can I wait?"

"You can," says Bhagwan, smiling, "but your heart wants a mala." Everyone cracks up, because Lawrie really is massaging his heart. I laugh and cry. Lawrie grins and nods. He becomes Deva Saguna, complete with mala.

"Deva means divine, Saguna means with form," Bhagwan tells him. "Your mother's name is Nirgun. Nirgun means formless. I have given your mother the name Nirgun because form comes from the formless. This whole world comes from the formless. The original source is formless and millions of forms arise from it. So the formless is the mother and with the form is the son. So between you two, it is complete."

Saguna gropes his way back to his seat, blinded by tears. We hug silently.

Colleen has been moving restlessly beside me, and when her name is called she leaps over the three front rows as if springloaded, landing plop! like a giant frog in front of Bhagwan. Everyone laughs, Bhagwan chuckles and slips the mala over her head.

"You may be the first person I have given sannyas to without asking," he tells her. "And this will be your new name: Ma Deva Turanti.

Deva means divine, and Turanti means quick; one who approaches
the divine quickly . . . Something to say?"

Turanti hesitates, then stammers, "I was going to tell you that I am
full of anger." I lean forward to hear the answer; anger is my Achilles'
heel too.

"Full of anger? Nothing is wrong in it. Anger simply means energy
stuck. Not finding a way to move, to be creative. When energy is stuck
it becomes stale, poisonous. It is just like a river. When it is not flowing it becomes dirty, stale, angry.

"A person who has no anger has nothing to grow with. He is impotent, dull, he has no intelligence. Anger is pure fuel. It can be used in
many ways. So dance, meditate—and you have to be quick! You have
to be true to your name, Turanti!"

With the coming of Saguna and Turanti my life shifted into overdrive. They came every morning for discourse, we ate breakfast together, and for days we tried to find a way for them to move out of the
hideous Green Hotel. One morning I was clearing away the rubble of
construction on the roof of Jesus House when the Indian contractor
spoke to me.

"Sorry it takes so long to finish your room," he said. "Two weeks more, it will be done."

I looked at him blankly. What room? "Your name is Nirgun, yes? Then this room we have built is for you. Laxmi has said it, this morning." He led me across the roof and flung open the door. A door into the most exotic room I have ever seen. An enormous room, totally bare. High, high ceilings, sparkling mosaic floor. A huge window-wall looked out on the feathery gulmohar tree, its bright orange blossoms flashing against a forest of green. And off the entrance of the room I glimpsed a bathroom! All my own!

I remembered how I'd insisted on a large room. Now my son was here, and so was the room. It smacked of magic. The room was big enough for all of us! I didn't ask questions, just installed Saguna and Turanti the same day, with only a futon and an enormous pot of elephant ear. They relaxed, glowing, not minding a bit that carpenters were still coming in and out.

Two weeks later the contractor told me the big room was finished, and I moved in with them; another sannyasin would need the turret room.

They asked me to write Bhagwan: could they have the tiny turret room? I hesitated, thinking perhaps they should write themselves.

"You're such a miracle worker, Nirgun," Turanti prompted, so I picked up my pen. Two days later Saguna read out the answer: "It is fine for Saguna and Turanti to live in the ashram. You should all flow together in the same room."

Flow together in the same room! I saw Turanti freeze into an ice cube so solid not even her hot anger could melt it. The blood drained from her face, her lips pinched tight, her stare scalded; hatred oozed from every pore. I couldn't blame her. They'd lived in the room for two weeks, just the two of them, and she had come to feel it was *her* room! Having to share it with a mother-in-law was too hideous to contemplate; I knew I would have felt the same. But Turanti desperately wanted to stay in the ashram. She knew from sannyasin gossip that hundreds were living outside the gates, many in makeshift huts by the river, hoping desperately that they would be invited to move in.

I had a screen made. Not a light airy affair of rice paper and bamboo, this screen was solid, dark, heavy. It spoiled the open beauty of the room, but it gave us all some privacy.

Saguna built a long, wide loft of solid teak with matching cupboards underneath. Turanti draped it with a yellow batik and put flowering plants in every corner and nook. We invited friends, and Turanti beamed when they exclaimed at the beauty of the room. But these moments of softening were rare. Venom lurked just beneath the surface. Turanti's face remained tight, closed.

Saguna threw himself into the groups that were springing up. Leaders of therapies from all over the world were coming to the ashram, drawn by the power of these new meditations to dig out the deep roots of repressed anger and fear and to help troubled twentieth century man understand his angst. Many therapists took sannyas and moved to Poona, bringing their own skills to share.

At the end of each group they all came to darshan to report and to receive guidance from Bhagwan. A new hybrid was created: existential therapy.

Saguna enrolled in Enlightenment Intensive, a three-day Zen style marathon with rotating partners, asking and answering only one question: "Who am I?" He did the Encounter group and came home looking shaken but joyful. Then he took part in Tantra, a group designed to help participants become at ease with their sexual nature.

"Tonight do the thing you fear most," the group leader suggested. Saguna asked Turanti if he could bring another girl home for the night, experiment with a threesome. Her face turned pale, but she agreed. I slept outside on the roof, angry when I found they'd locked me out of the bathroom. Next morning Turanti looked even tighter, paler.

Saguna went into a three-week residential Vipassana group. While he was away, without warning Turanti brought home a lover.

My hands clenched into fists as I lay rigid in my narrow bed, listening. There was no escape from the pleasure noises coming from the loft across the room—panting, moans, the creak of boards. I stared up into the stifling Indian night, watching waves of anger wash over me.

I was here to meditate, to find myself, not to listen to these moans that jarred me like a nail scratching across a blackboard. Cries that Turanti did not try to stifle as she did when making love to Saguna. I knew she wanted me to hear, wanted to shock me.

Rigid sexual attitudes still clung to my psyche like warm saran wrap. A childhood in rough frontier country had left scars. . . .

Age ten, on the school steps, a hand between my legs. My body froze, my legs clamped; the boy's fingers probed, worked upward. Sweat broke out on the back of my neck. If I made a ruckus he'd get a terrible beating from Dad, I'd be an outcast in the school forever.

I moved. He followed. The school bell rang.

Alone on the farm, age fourteen, a logger grabbed me. I pushed him away and he shoved me down, dragged my right arm up behind my back; pain shot through my body. He started to pull my jeans off. In a voice so strong I didn't recognize it as mine I said, "Eddie, if you let me go now, I won't tell Father."

The cruel grip on my arm relaxed. Eddie disappeared.

Age eighteen, a date with a naval officer. He fumbled in his urgency, squeezing my breasts, his rough tongue in my mouth, pushing. I willed myself to relax, to let my body respond, and it did respond—with nausea. I threw up in the rhododendrons at the front of the house.

Twenty-two years old, coming out of my sexual ice pack with a patient lover. Parking, kissing, cuddling. A month, two months. Slowly, slowly his hand moved up my leg, alert to stop or retreat at the slightest sign of resistance. My body began to thaw, to come alive. A marvellous warmth spread through me as he caressed my breasts, lovingly. Four months, five months—his hand between my legs. My body exploded into wave after wave of joy. Every cell on fire, juices flooding out, flesh and spirit together in a wholeness beyond time.

Now on my tiny couch, listening to the intimate, ecstatic noises from the loft, filled with soft memories of sex and joy, my body melted with a new tenderness. Turanti was shaking off the shackles of her moral upbringing, just as I had.

In that soft relaxed state, other memories surfaced.

My own experience had shown me that the bondage of exclusive love brings about the need to break free. . . .

When I met Glen Hamilton, a fellow social worker, the magic of love engulfed me. Sweetness welling up from nowhere, spreading; dissolving, merging, wanting nothing more from life, ever, than *this*.

We had a great marriage, Glen and I, by any standard. I got pregnant on a deerskin rug on our honeymoon in Depoe Bay, Oregon. Our firstborn, Craig, could have answered an ad for the world's most troublefree, happy baby, and I flowed into the joys of mothering. Blair arrived as planned the next year, and two years later came Lawrie/ Saguna, another happy accident.

Glen and I took part-time jobs and threw our energy into a flower farm on Vancouver Island, peopled it with Dolly the dog, Sassy the cat, a pony, a pet goat and sheep, a skunk, an owl, a wounded peregrine falcon; thirty guinea pigs, and a guest, Harry the crow.

One spring afternoon the phone rang. It was Mr. Darkes, the principal of Royal Oak Elementary. He didn't seem to know quite how to put it. "It's just that—well, your crow follows the boys to school every day and, uh, he does make a mess of the teachers' cars. And today, well, you see, he's just flown off with a check from my desk."

Hysterical laughter rose in my throat.

"I'm so sorry that he . . . that he . . . about the mess on their cars," I finally managed to gasp. "But you see, he's not my crow, he's not anyone's crow! He just hangs out in the tree here, flies anywhere he wants."

"Is there any way he could be kept in a cage?" Mr. Darkes asked gently. Anger flooded through me. I hung up, unable to talk to him. Wanting me to cage Harry, for God's sake. A free, funny crow!

I went out to the garden and asked myself, what's the matter with me? I'm feeling angry, frustrated. Why?

Glen and I had built this perfect life, a healthy, happy family in a back-to-nature paradise. We fit so close together. The first wild ecstasy had settled into a quiet trust with lots of good sex. The bonds that held our family together went deep.

Nothing is missing, I thought wryly.

Except change.

And challenge.

And *freedom*.

Harry the Crow was more free. He could fly with the kids to school, or sit in the tree all day. He could even shit on teachers' cars if he felt like it. I couldn't even say "shit" to a teacher on the phone. Why couldn't I use a plain Anglo-Saxon word if I wanted?

"Anything wrong, honey?" Glen asked me later. But I couldn't tell him my vision of the farm, the family, as a trap. He'd be hurt beyond words. And how could words help? There was no way to alter the brutal choice: family or freedom.

Now in Poona, lying in my small bed, listening to the orgasmic noises in the loft, I felt the same impotence. Knowing this would break Saguna's heart if he found out. Knowing he *would* find out: Turanti had tasted the joy of freedom and would not easily put that joy aside.

Next day I went to the river. I had to get out in the open, to look at a feeling I now saw had been growing inside me, a feeling I'd had so often before: stifled, imprisoned, wanting to break free.

Free from what?

Slowly it came to me that my loss of freedom was self-inflicted.

I was a prisoner of my own silence.

Bhagwan had ridiculed monks who sat in caves for years on end, coming out as angry as when they went in. Had this been a message for me?

I came back to the ashram and browsed in the bookstore, looking for his discourse on the monks. Instead I came across a recent picture of myself taken at darshan. It was a shocker. *Me* in *my* monk role: homespun robe with high cowl neck, straggling hair and uneven bangs, huge horn-rimmed glasses; a grim, forbidding, tight-lipped face.

I stared at it, unbelieving. And suddenly knew that my silence had become yet another trap, cutting me off from freedom to change, to grow, to explore the new.

When Saguna finished his group he bounded into the room, gave me a great hug and said, "Mom, don't you think two years is long enough? You don't know what you're missing. I think you should come out of silence and do the encounter group."

I broke into a great grin.

Sitting in front of Bhagwan in darshan . . . "One part of me feels really good, that things are going great," I tell him. "But when I look at what I'm doing, it doesn't seem great at all. I see the same impatience, the same need to control, the same anger, the same carelessness; they keep coming up. One of my roommates says maybe I'm stuck, I should come out of silence and do the encounter group. So that's my question. Should I do a group, and is this sense of well-being just my mind playing tricks?"

Bhagwan tells me, "No, no, nothing, it is really happening. On the whole you feel a very great well-being, a very great silence and happiness; and still somewhere in a dark corner of the heart some problems can go on creating their noise. There is nothing wrong in it. Man is vast!"

My whole body/mind relaxes. I've been expecting another hit.

He goes on. "And sometimes it happens that the more silent you become, the more aware you become of the contradictions. It is as if the whole room is dirty, then you clean a part of it. Because of the clean part, now the whole room looks very dirty. When this clean part was not there, when the whole room was dirty, you were not aware of it. It is just as if on a plain wall you throw black ink; it becomes so clear and loud.

"Your silence is absolutely authentic. Ordinarily one lives in such a turmoil, in such a noisy mind, then you cannot be aware. Now you can be aware.

"But a group can still be good. Encounter will be perfect, do encounter, mmmmm? And in the group come out of silence. After the group you can go into silence again: we will see first. Because silence has not to be there for your whole life. If your energy starts feeling that it would be good to come out, you can come out."

So it came to pass that I signed up for Encounter. Then I gave my rusty vocal chords a workout, posting a sign on our door: **BEWARE! SCREAMING PRACTICE 4:30 TO 5:30**.

In a jubilant, boisterous mood. Encounter was known as the roughest, toughest group in the ashram, meant to break through the strongest defenses of those willing to risk. A challenge to any pioneer.

Chapter 6

Encounter

C HAITANYA CHAMBER, where the Encounter Group happened, was next to our new cafeteria. But it was underground, down a narrow flight of stairs, through a dim corridor lined with closed doors: Claustrophobic. The whole place oozed darkness and secrecy, a space suited for digging into our murky unconscious.

As the group room door opened, a blast of hot sweaty air struck me in the face. No windows. The walls were lined floor to ceiling with thick brown padding; the room was in fact one big padded cell. Except for a pile of thin blue mattresses and a box of foam bats and boxing gloves, the space loomed stark and bare.

"Stark and bare" described the group showers too. Everyone going into the bathroom for the first time shrank back. The room had been designed around a theme: *no place to hide*. A naked square space, mercilessly lit with fluorescent lights that glared off the white-tiled floors and walls. Along one side ran a row of modern Western toilets, with no seats. No stalls around them.

On the opposite side of the room were the showers: no walls, no curtains. You took a shower staring across at a person taking a shit. You took a shit staring at a person taking a shower. And when you brushed your teeth at the center sinks, you took your choice.

Instructions from Teertha, the group leader, were brief: No one is to leave without permission. Meals will be sent in three times a day. Let it all hang out.

A great urge to let out my own aggressive impulses road roughshod over the habits of a lifetime. For seven days, whatever came to me to do I did on the instant, without stopping to think.

A burly Indian introduced himself as "Raj", an Indian Army colonel. He told us he was worried about the small size of his prick.

"Let's have a look," I said to him, and persuaded him to lie on the floor so we could examine it. Other women joined in: we stretched him out, pulled off his pants and his underpants, checked his penis. More women joined us, examining, exclaiming, eyes gleaming. I felt the rising excitement: *Now I'm the one with the hand between the legs!* Like a flock of harpies, feeling the safety of numbers, curious, eager, we women did what men had always done to us—but gently. We talked together, agreed Raj didn't need an operation.

We told him his prick was perfectly okay.

Suddenly aware of a spark of anger toward the handsome girl with a mane of curling dark hair kneeling next to me, I challenged her to a wrestling match. A pack of male muscles disguised in female form, she pinned me down within seconds. I managed to free one hand, wind it in her long hair, and pull. Really pull. Swept by a glorious vengeful madness, acting out the hurt of a lifetime of hair traumas. Not all her pounding and squeezing could shake me loose, not even when she kicked me with all the force of her long strong legs. We rolled over and over on the floor, screaming and swearing. Others watched and applauded, and our screams faded into exhausted laughter.

We lay against the wall for a bit, still in each other's arms, not talking. By some strange alchemy, the energy of anger flowed into its opposite. For both of us the urge to hit became the urge to hug.

A lot of what happened in Encounter wasn't dramatic. Just standing in a group with our clothes off, just seeing all these naked bodies, getting easy with our own, thinking nothing of it—the only naked bodies many of us had seen had been our lovers, and that was usually in the dark. It was so easy and such fun, just looking, talking, relaxing.

Amazed, I found myself enjoying being hugged by perfect strangers; amazed again at how quickly the touch of a hand could change a stranger into a friend. And how easily my hands could soothe or revive my own spirits, massaging the body I'd always despised, enjoying its curves and angles. Touching and being touched created an orgasmic sense of joining, of melting into others and into myself.

Teertha had a comic streak. When a wordsmith went on and on about her ascetic, virginal path and the rest of us sat in total boredom, I glanced at Teertha, willing him to do something. And he was doing something. We were all naked at the time, sitting against the walls. He was sitting in a corner playing with his mala, draping it over his penis. I whooped with delight. As everyone caught onto the act, the monologue drowned in a storm of laughter. Everyone knew that Bhagwan, unlike other mystics, insists that you have to go through sex, not repress it, in order to go beyond it.

The British actor Terence Stamp was in the group, and to me he seemed to have "gone beyond." Almost every female in the room tried her luck at seducing him. It was obvious to me that he wasn't into that space, that he'd been there too often. But they kept trying. When Teertha declared a master/slave night—the slave to do everything the master ordered—women made a beeline for Terence, and he made a beeline for me.

"Shall we go out for dinner," he said. We traded the sweaty surroundings of a mad padded cell for the overripe opulence of the Blue Diamond, a five-star restaurant close to the ashram. My senses were strangely heightened: pink light flashing on ornate English silverware, soft fold of pink napkins, the tinkle of ice in my water glass, all came to vivid life.

So did stories of his film career, and my avid interest kept us talking for hours. A simple delight in human conversation, forgotten in two long years of silence, washed over me, washed away all memory of why we were there.

The moment was enough.

As the group went on, the driving urge to act out my aggression faded. When a German man told me I reminded him of the mother he hated, my first impulse was to ignore, avoid, deflect his remark. All my life I had run away from hostility. At the faintest breath of trouble in a public encounter I grabbed the oil and started pouring. In that instant I became aware of what a coward I really was. My aggression had always been undercover; it turned tail and ran when attacked.

It came to me now to face up to this man's aggressiveness, to let mine off the leash entirely. I didn't *feel* at all aggressive, *but a wave is coming, I'm going to ride that wave.*

"So what were you doing to your mother?" I sneer, eyebrows rising suggestively. "Maybe she should have beaten you harder. You Nazis are all motherfuckers at heart."

Wolfgang pushes me down on the floor, pins my arms and beats me with German efficiency, striking my legs and thighs with his fists and elbows, slapping my face, over and over. As if I were one of the onlookers I watch my body respond—spitting, swearing, laughing. I can still see the faces in the room like a remembered movie: faces full of fear (he may kill her!) uncertainty (should I try to stop him?) anger (why doesn't someone *do* something!) and just plain voyeur fascination. Teertha stays expressionless, alert.

Wolfgang stops of his own accord.

That night he runs a fever, wants to leave the group, but Teertha persuades him to stay.

"It happens often when you get into deep stuff," he tells him. "You'll be fine in the morning."

It feels as natural to mother him as it had to taunt him. I bring him extra blankets, bring my own blankets and curl up beside him; fetch him ice cold water in the night. He's fine in the morning. And so am I—my body a mass of bruises but inside I feel light, airy. As if some ancient burdens have fallen away.

And they had. I came out of the group feeling warm and feminine. I had experienced my body being woman-weak, totally helpless, and had found a fearlessness that amazed me.

With this new fearlessness, the aggression that had been so much a part of my nature seemed to fade, as if I no longer needed to fight to prove my strength.

I saw how phony was the femininity I'd once mimicked: the wigs, the false tan, the provocative dresses. I saw them as weapons I'd used to equal the odds in the battle of the sexes, weapons no longer needed.

Now I felt strong in myself—a different strength than the physical strength of men, more passive; more like the power of a blade of grass that bows down to the wind.

The change must have showed, because one of the women in the group brought me two robes, a simple orange velvet and a delicate swirling chiffon. I put the harsh homespun away forever.

This change showed outwardly, but the most important change did not. Only I knew that for moments together in that seven days I had lived in a space—in the body but not of it—from which I could watch what was happening. Without thought, without feeling.

Chapter 7

Ego Bashing

*B*UT I HAD MORE encountering to do, this time in my own
room. Of all the devices Bhagwan concocted to shatter our set
life patterns, the most powerful for me was telling Turanti, Saguna and
me to "flow together in the same room."

Turanti projected onto me her feelings toward her Catholic con-
vent-reared mother. Neither sex nor any other feeling had been up for
discussion in her family home. They'd lived on the surface, just as I
had done, in a never-never land of pretend. Now Turanti had to live
with another mother figure.

My coming out of silence didn't help. Years later she told me,
"Suddenly you emerged as Puck the Sprite, wafting around in kaftans
and silk robes, with all this crazy energy. I hated it."

Slowly, slowly she began to feel the weight of her own armor.
Terrified of cathartic groups, she wrote to Bhagwan, pouring out her
irrational hatred of me, her anger at having to share the room. "Should
I do the encounter? Or primal? I hate the idea, but I can't go on like
this."

Between sending her letter and getting Bhagwan's reply, Turanti saw our situation in a different light. "Just seeing my responsibility, taking a risk, offering to do what I most feared—something has changed," she told me, "as if I've stepped back. It's easy to see how I've been dumping my past hates on you. When you were in silence I could project anything I liked on you. You've been my mattress to beat, my blank wall to scribble swear words on.

"I don't have to do encounter. We've had a group going right here."

The reply from Bhagwan confirmed her own inner voice: "No need to do encounter; primal only if you want to."

Then existence supplied a great let-go for Turanti. She came down with hepatitis. Bhagwan has called hepatitis a "spiritual" disease because it leaves the person totally vulnerable, defenseless, wide open to whatever comes.

"And what came my way," Turanti told me, "was an ocean of loving care. You gave me sponge baths, clean sheets, and *orange juice*. Liters of fresh orange juice, squeezed by hand; the only food I could absorb. Memories of my own mother flooded back, soft memories, grateful memories; memories that had been smothered to near extinction.

"You had put me in your bed, and just lying there I saw how the big heavy screen shut each of us into a corner; your space was no bigger than the tiny cell you had before. One day I asked, glancing at the screen, keeping my voice casual, 'Do you think we could get rid of this?'

"You looked at me, and ran out. And within minutes you were back with Akbar and the two of you wrestled the huge beast outside; I felt bad that I couldn't help. Then you came back breathing hard, with this huge grin, and I laughed. You fell onto the bed and hugged me and I hugged you back, and suddenly we were both crying."

We didn't know it then, but Turanti's most intense group would be her work in the ashram. She and Saguna returned to Canada to earn money for a room of their own.

While they were away, my second son Blair arrived with his 14-month-old son Kelly. They stayed in my room, and my heart melted, just watching the loving care with which he bathed and changed the child. Like me, Blair is not one to pour out his feelings and I didn't pry into his marriage. The two of them took sannyas, and Bhagwan gave Kelly a name that means "love diamond."

Blair's wife came a week later and took sannyas. While they did a couples group I baby-sat my love diamond grandchild, taking him everywhere. In Sufi dancing he put his right shoulder in and his right shoulder out in time to the music and the dancers cracked up. Everyone adored him.

Blair, his wife and Kelly went back to the West and dropped sannyas within months. Turanti and Saguna came back and moved in with me again; no other rooms were available. The numbers of Western visitors had increased tenfold and all ashram residents now worked full-time, without pay but getting free food and housing.

Saguna went to the woodworking shop; he was ecstatic. Turanti was sent to the job she most feared: the kitchen. Charged with feeding the hungry hundreds who were maintaining and expanding the ashram, plus the crowds of visitors, it was the most dreaded work placement in the ashram.

Physically The Kitchen resembled the Christian picture of hell, dark and smoky, with kerosene stoves that flamed up erratically and hissed loudly, threatening to explode, blackening the walls with their fumes.

Deeksha, the fat Italian mamma who ran The Kitchen, had earned a reputation as a tyrant. Bhagwan called her his Zen sword, and sometimes sent sannyasins to her with instructions to surrender.

"It is difficult, I know, that's why it has to be done. She is going to be your master for a few days," he told them. "It is easy to surrender to me, it is not so easy to surrender to Deeksha."

"Surrender" has a very specific meaning in Bhagwan's vocabulary. "Surrender" and "obedience" are diametrically opposed. Obedience is the greatest sin. Listen to your own inner voice, obey it. Surrender only your prickly ego, that conditioned part of you that clings to the past, to habits, to past ideas about how things should be.

I had learned about devices to shatter the ego from Gurdjieff, who treated the ego as a simple case of mistaken identity: the belief that I am my personality. The word personality comes from Latin 'persona', meaning mask. The mask is thick, built up over a lifetime from the opinions of mother-father-relatives-friends-teachers-preachers.

But how to shatter the mask?

In 1973 the absurd antics of E. J. Gold and the Institute for the Development of Harmonious Human Beings had drawn me to his workshops in Crestline, California. There, old ways of seeing and doing met shock after shock.

Day and night we painted his lovely home in this posh mountain resort, urged awake after only an hour of sleep; painting white latex over mellow rosewood walls, turning the gracious house into an ersatz spaceship. Many dropped out of the workshop rather than drop their reverence for that mellow glow.

We played monopoly for thirty-six consecutive hours. Listened for hours to hard rock superimposed on a screaming Pentecostal minister. Once we were given the chance of breaking any old habit. For twenty-four hours I tried not to push my glasses up my nose. Do anything else, take them off, replace them, but no pushing. Not once did I catch myself in time.

These exercises showed me how immeasurably strong are the chains of habit. How could anyone break them?

That Bhagwan used Deeksha's kitchen as a device to help sannyasins break old habits wasn't news to me. I'd learned about it long before Turanti was sent there.

"I'm one of Deeksha's favorites," a lanky hippy friend from Toronto told me. "She loves to yell at me. She takes one look around the kitchen and sees half the people chopping vegetables mechanically, like zombies. When she screams and yells, she knows everyone's going to wake up."

"How do you cope with it?" I asked him.

"I was real upset in the beginning. I wrote Bhagwan, and he said 'Next time you feel like crying, laugh instead.'

"And I did, the very next time she yelled at me. That changed everything. She just walked away and never yelled at me in the same way again. And now she's putting in the new marble counters I asked for!"

A huge grin lightened his face." It's *such* a meditation. Washing pots is such a good one. There's only thirty pots, all sizes, different kinds of metal, and a few scrubbies. That's it. You're in this room, you're there every day, and all you do is wash the fucking pots."

He laughed uproariously. "That's all you're doing, scrubbing away on the pot that someone's just burned. You're feeling like a piece of pigshit, just horrible, and you're wondering *How am I going to get out of here? I'll have to call home, they'll send me money for a ticket. I'm not going to stay. I'll give it one more day, maybe, just one more day.* And then maybe six hours later you're scrubbing away at a pot and you're thinking, *Shit, this is great! I've got such an easy job. And suddenly. Hey, wait a minute. That same pot came by six hours ago and I was going to leave!*

"So it's a meditation, right? For me, meditation happens when there's a fixed point that let's me see how my mind moves in relation to it. The pots are fixed, the situation is exactly the same—and my mind is all over the place! And I can see it, *really* see it!"

What was Turanti supposed to see? Every day in the kitchen Deeksha hit her with shock after shock.

"There's this mountain of tomatoes in this big pot, and I have to stir and stir. If they burn you're in deep shit," Turanti told me. "So I stir and sweat as if my life depended on it—and it really feels like that. The other cooks are running around with the same look of panic. Even if we aren't working we try to look busy. Deeksha has this way of materializing right behind you, she hits you with a *thali* or a saucepan or a spoon.

"I can't even make a sandwich to please her. They're always 'too theek, too theen, too late!'" She mimicked Deeksha's strident Italian accent.

Even knowing that Deeksha was a device to help kitchen workers break out of lifetime habits, fully aware of her own repressed anger, Turanti still reacted with ill-concealed fury. She stormed around our room each morning before work, slammed out the door. But to Deeksha she showed only her frozen white face.

Deeksha wielded her Zen stick even more ferociously.

"You are not fit to peel vegetables!" she sneered at Turanti. "From now on you will be a cleaner!"

She spilled her cup of chai onto the floor and said, "Wipe it up!"

"Her eyes blazed such a challenge. The idea of wiping a floor that someone else has slopped on, the humiliation of it!" Turanti choked, telling me about it. "A huge **FUCK YOU DEEKSHA** roars up in my guts, and sticks in my throat. Deeksha's energy is so immense: I dare you! I dare you to be angry! And I don't dare. I don't dare to be angry. I go and get a mop."

The Zen stick struck with even greater force.

"You are a rock, a stone, you 'ave no feelings!" Deeksha yelled. "The only time your energy moves is when you see a penis! You don't deserve to live in this ashram, I will see that you are thrown out! Go and see Laxmi, now!"

"When Laxmi asks me if I have something to say, I shake my head," Turanti told me. "But suddenly tears start flooding down my cheeks. They just pour down. I can't speak, I look her in the eyes and send out a silent plea. *Please, Laxmi, don't send me away. Here I'm alive, can't you see? I'm just starting to come alive! Don't send me away.*"

The sight of frozen Turanti melting in a torrent of tears, her face flushed with fierce emotion, pleading for understanding, was enough. Laxmi heard the message. She sent Turanti, still in tears, back to Deeksha for another chance.

Deeksha also heard.

"Deeksha's put me in charge of the handymen—fourteen of them!" Turanti's face was pink, glowing. The glow stayed with her, day after day. New buildings were going up everywhere. She pushed her all-male crew to the limit, coaxing, flirting, challenging. "Something's changed, Nirgun," she told me. "After twelve or thirteen hours I'm still flying high!"

As Turanti's energy took off in her new job, she split up with Saguna in an explosion of anger, fear, and grief.

"Saguna's so possessive," she confided one day, "He wants a one-woman/one-man relationship. And now I don't want it. I'm feeling attracted to other men—especially my Divine Apronwasher." She pointed him out as he hung out aprons on our glorious sparkling roof, naked in the sun, tall and muscled with shocks of curly black hair.

"'Follow your feelings' seems to be what the commune is all about," I told her. "We both know what happens if you sit on them."

Even as I spoke I couldn't believe my words. I was actually encouraging the beloved of my youngest son to follow her own feelings, knowing the terrible anguish it would cause Saguna—he who had been the only son at home, helping me through the hellish months of my own marriage breakup. . . .

The breakup had been long and painful. Before we married, Glen had asked for an "open" marriage. I was shocked, but agreed. So when I fell in love I felt no guilt about taking a lover.

Driving home one day from Lighthouse Park, my feelings played themselves out again. My lover's fingers brushing the hair of my arm, the goose pimples rising where he touched; my whole being drowning in a joy that seemed not of this world; my body melting, disappearing. I pulled off the road and sat, trembling, for long minutes.

The joy died away. In its wake came a cool clarity: *How this will end doesn't matter. Nothing could make me regret these moments.*

Perhaps the certainty made me careless; Glen came to know.

"Does this change the way you feel about us?" he asked.

"No," I told him, honestly. "I love you, I want to stay married to you. But I've fallen in love and I'm coping the best I know how."

He seemed satisfied. But when I came home late one afternoon with tiny scratches on my arms from the blackberry bushes, he turned white. "You're still seeing him!" That moment marked the real end of our marriage.

Glen fell in love with his secretary. "You must have noticed. I dream about her, wake up in the night."

Shock waves of jealousy flooded my body; from toes to tongue they gripped me in a paralyzing force. *Had I put Glen through this?*

"Tell her how you feel," I stammered.

Kay didn't want to threaten her marriage. For two years we lived in limbo. Then her husband died. Glen was still in love; I suggested we buy a summer place close to hers. Wouldn't his yearning fade when satisfied, as mine had?

This time she fell into his arms.

He told me about it one night as we lay side by side, not touching. Burning cold on a warm summer night, I managed to get out "You'll be wanting a divorce, then?" To my surprise and joy he said, "Why can't I have you both?"

There's still a chance for us, I gloated. Great notions of freedom had long since evaporated. Just let me hang onto my man, for better for worse, till death us do part!

For a year we tried to fit our marriage around Kay. Finally we separated. The day he moved out, Glen gave me one of his old-time big hugs and whispered, "I couldn't have done this without you."

My first six months without a mate was a time of sackcloth and ashes and valium. I slept alone in a king-size bed with purple satin sheets, mourning twenty years of sleeping spoon fashion. Lawrie, not yet Saguna, still lived at home. One night I let my grief out in bellows of anguish; he overcame his no-touch conditioning and came in to cradle me like a baby, stroking my hair, letting his tears flow with mine.

Now I was encouraging his beloved to follow her feelings for another man. What kind of a mother was I? But the sense of rightness remained. Love without freedom is not love at all.

What happens if you *don't* sit on your feelings? Turanti told me about it, breathlessly:

"Saguna is at work, and the Divine Apronwasher and I are on a mattress in the warm sun, naked. Suddenly I look up and Saguna is there, ten feet away, standing on the roof at the top of the stairs, his hands against the door jambs. His face is white, even his lips. I can see the pulse throbbing in his throat.

"I'm afraid of him; he's been doing karate for years. He goes into our room and comes back with my mala. He tears it apart, the beads scatter over my head and shoulders. Then he attacks his punching bag, roaring his rage, cursing me with every vile word. The roof shakes. The apronwasher escapes.

"I run to the nearest room and hide under the blankets, trying to shut out the pounding, the curses. I'm terrified, I know I can't go back. I have nowhere to stay, no money of my own, no support of any kind. And as I crouch there naked, through the terror I feel a calmness, a lightness I have never known."

Saguna asked to have a darshan that night; Turanti and I went too. He was haggard, sleepless, red-eyed.

Sitting in front of Bhagwan, tears flood from his eyes. The darshan diary records that he "looked like Christ crucified." I cry openly. Saguna pours his heart out, holding nothing back—the sense of betrayal, the incredible pain.

And Bhagwan tells him to be grateful to the woman!

It is so absurd, so unexpected. Beside me Turanti starts to cry. Saguna begins to laugh through his tears. Seeing him laugh, others join in. Be grateful—such a preposterous idea. But Bhagwan explains it.

"This is how one drops clinging, possessiveness, jealousy. These are all childish things, they don't matter. Whether you see your woman making love to somebody in a dream or in reality is not in fact any way different. You are in both cases just the observer.

"When you see your woman making love to another man, it is so painful it helps you to be detached, to watch," he tells Saguna. "It is like in an emergency ward. Those who are badly wounded, their wounds are almost mortal, you will see: they are detached, just observing what is happening. In such moments you cannot identify with your feelings.

"Never miss the opportunity that a shock brings; use that opportunity to grow."

When we came out of darshan, Saguna and Turanti hugged for long wordless minutes. He put up a tent for her on a quiet corner of the roof, laid a carpet outside, built a teak cupboard for her clothes.

Afterward the three of us stayed best friends. United in the resolve to follow our own intelligence, our own hearts, not repressing. Whether our feelings led to cries of ecstasy or screams of agony mattered not at all.

My aggressiveness, Turanti's fears, Saguna's jealousy all came to their full peak and began to die naturally on the vine, making way for something new.

Chapter 8

Home of the Gods?

TWO YEARS AFTER I came to Poona, Laxmi appeared at the door of my room in Jesus House.

"Nirgun, Laxmi needs to know if you would wish to come to Lao Tzu House and clean, in the daytimes?"

Clean in Lao Tzu! Clean in the master's house, so close to him, the highest favor. A ripple of laughter in my belly swelled to a tidal wave of joy. Laxmi read the ecstatic "Yes!" in my eyes, and smiled.

LaoTzu House, a huge mansion set among flowering shrubs and trees, was off limits to all but a few who lived or had business there. Of the residents only Vivek, who was on call for 24-hours a day as Bhagwan's caregiver, could bring in a friend or a lover.

The high wrought iron gate of Lao Tzu stood ajar during the day, but inside sat a guard, day and night. A storm of angry protest had been roused by Bhagwan's scathing censure of politicians and priests in lectures to huge audiences around India. This anger was to escalate and lead to attempts on his life. Sannyasins saw their master as a pre-

cious treasure and guarded him zealously, armed only with awareness.
I watched my ego rise and preen itself as I came in through the gate as
a cleaner: the rush of pride as the guard studied the list and nodded me
through; the greater thrill when he no longer looked at the list; the
envious stares of sannyasins who witnessed my easy coming and going through the sacred portal.

Within a month nobody took any notice—including me. But an
undercurrent of gratefulness flowed through each and every day.

Lao Tzu House, an old mansion from the time of the British Raj,
had high sloping ceilings—I had to fetch a ladder to reach them with a
cobweb broom. Its cream walls and simple granite staircase were bare,
bland. I hadn't expected the old-fashioned simplicity, nor the silence!
The great house was filled with it. Not a dead silence, it rang with joy.
Smiles shone in the eyes of those who passed wordlessly in the corridors.

"Don't be sad and don't be serious," Bhagwan told us in discourse.
"That is not the way to commune with a master. You are bridged only
by rejoicing. Real joy is not feverish, it is cool, it is very silent. It sings
a song, but the song is that of silence."

Working in Lao Tzu I tasted again the same silent communing
that filled the vast empty spaces of my childhood.

Only Bhagwan's care-giver, Vivek, entered his room when he was
there. He never went out of his room alone. She escorted him to meals
in his small dining room, to discourses and to darshan, guarding his
privacy with the fierce devotion of a lion mother. None of the rest of us
glimpsed him by day or night, except his secretary, doctor, dentist,
and robemakers, who saw him by appointment.

I cleaned the upstairs rooms and a corridor that ran through the
house, a ribbon of tiny concrete squares painted dull red. Nirupa, a
wide-eyed innocent blonde from Toronto, cleaned the other rooms,
worked in the garden. She taught me the art of cleaning without a
vacuum, shared her precious Western scrubbies with me, and laughed
away my upstairs cleaning problems.

I cleaned Mukta's room. Mukta took special care of Bhagwan's
gardens, checking the trees for rot, mucking about in the swan's new
pool, keeping an eagle eye on her eager staff. "Don't prune *anything!*
Bhagwan wants them to grow naturally," I heard her tell them fiercely,
and the garden grew in luxurious disorder.

But in Mukta's room, order was god. The gleaming teak shelves displayed delicate objets d'art, artistically arranged; they were to be put back exactly in place after dusting. Bred to carefree housekeeping, now I had to bring total attention to the task at hand, sweating each time lest I forget.

If Mukta was meticulous, Teertha was a tyrant. Almost invisible marks on the floor were to show me exactly where his desk, bed and chair were to be replaced. I'm short-sighted, and many minutes each day were spent scrabbling on hands and knees to find the precious marks, till Nirupa's laughter at my tale overwhelmed my paranoia. Then I laughed too. Teertha had arranged his furniture to correspond exactly with the bed, desk and chair of Bhagwan in the room beneath!

One day when buds were beginning to burst out on the huge trees inside the gate, Vivek asked me to help spring-clean Bhagwan's room. The stark simplicity startled me. An enormous bed with three great pillows, an exquisite rosewood stereo cabinet, a desk and chair. That was all.

Chetana, a tall dark-haired beauty from Cornwall, removed the curtains slowly, reverently, and swept off with them to his laundry. I caught glimpses of her there throughout the morning, up to her knees in an ecstasy of foaming soapsuds, her face radiant as a child let loose in a water arcade—a fairy child grown tall but still aglow with wonder.

I scrubbed the walls while Nirupa and his two robemakers worked on the heavy bed cover, made by stitching six Indian blankets together. The only bed covering Bhagwan ever used, they had to be unstitched, washed, dried and restitched all in one day. Though we worked in almost total silence I felt as intimate with my fellow workers as with old friends.

The shock of Bhagwan's bare room stayed with me. I knew he had a host of followers who would give him anything, and wild stories circulated in the Indian papers about the "sex guru". It was startling to find him living in such simplicity and solitude.

I'd come to understand Bhagwan's viewpoint on sex. His ideas were misunderstood and maligned, in the East and later in the West. In keeping with most spiritual traditions, he saw the need to transcend sex, but recognized that this must come through transformation, not repression.

"Sex is man's most vibrant energy, but it should not be an end in itself; sex should lead man to his soul," he said once in the early days. "Man cannot ordinarily reach the depths of his being that he reaches in the consummation of the sexual act; there man reaches beyond himself."

But the moment of ecstasy through sex is short-lived. "After every act of orgasm a man feels empty, drained—with a touch of heartburn. The desire is for something else, not physical gratification." If awareness is brought to the act, at some point sexual desire will drop away on its own. Leaders of religions, from Mahatma Ghandi to the Pope, have pushed humanity into an abyss of sex. By demanding that we repress something as natural as sex they have, Bhagwan charged, conspired to make the whole world a gigantic asylum. This natural urge has been degraded, labelled as passion, lust. Not so, he says; celibacy is the end, but man has to go through sex to go beyond it.

These words struck me with the hammer blow of truth.

Bhagwan didn't try to project an ascetic, saint-like image. On the contrary, his discourses were peppered with bawdy jokes. And cleaning his dining room table after his meal one day I was shocked and then delighted by the childlike abandon with which he ate.

Bhagwan insisted, "I am an ordinary human being, just like you." But sometimes he added, "The only difference is, I am awake and you are asleep." And that small difference set him a world apart from those of us around him. Every act—folding his hands, answering a question, rising, walking—conveyed the rapt awareness of a skier on an icy slope.

I was mopping the red corridor in Lao Tzu one morning with absurd delight when the kitchen door flew open and Vivek came out. Close-up, Vivek was arresting. Long dark hair with a fringe, pixie face, a pale complexion that had never seen the Indian sun. Her wide eyes were a strange blue/hazel, mysterious, alive. She put out a restrained energy; not hot energy like mine, hers was cool.

Vivek took my arm gently and pulled me through the door where only a special few entered: the inner sanctum where Bhagwan's food was prepared.

"Nirgun," she said, "Neera has just gone off with tendonitis. She's been helping me cook for Bhagwan, doing the veggies and keeping the kitchen clean. Could you fill in for her for three weeks?" Her soft English accent matched her appearance.

Could I? A rush of adrenaline nearly paralyzed my tongue. "I'd love to," I managed, cringing a little because the bottom of my robe was splashed with soapy water, my hands were rough and red. Vivek looked like a queen in a highnecked robe that clung to her exquisite figure. Her hands were graceful, white with long painted nails.

"Good!" She smiled a great wide smile, and my uneasiness dropped away. "Astha will be here in a minute to show you around. I have to see to Bugsy. Help yourself to a cup of chai." And she was off.

I stood in a daze, it had been so sudden. Torn between delight and shock: *Bugsy?!!*

I looked around the kitchen. Black and gray granite slabs covered the floor and the counter that ran the full length of the room. Huge papaya trees in the driveway shaded the windows. Through the branches I caught a glimpse of the orange Fire of the Forest. A cool, serene room—a single question came to me and it was anything but spiritual: for God's sake, where's the equipment?

The only stove in evidence was an old four-burner gas plate on the counter. An antique refrigerator stood near the door, a grinding machine in the far corner, a sink under the windows. Rows of pots and pans with rounded bottoms and flat covers sat on shelves under the counter, china cups and saucers on a wall shelf, and on the counter a *thali*, a huge round silver tray, held eight small dull silver bowls. I grabbed a cloth and started rubbing them.

Astha came in. She was young, tall, strongly built and couldn't have been more friendly. She told me the kitchen routine: Vivek takes Bhagwan's meals in at eleven in the morning and six at night. Always the same: a thali of dahl and vegetables, chutney and curd and chapatis, salad, fruit juice.

"That's it?" I asked incredulously.

"Vivek takes him a cup of tea every morning at six and a snack at bedtime," she told me. Astha had been working in his kitchen for years. I was impressed by the salads she made for Bhagwan; they were works of art—dramatic, showy.

In the next three weeks I dug into all the nooks and corners, a Canadian-pioneer springclean. Vivek came in one day while I was cleaning under the grinder and shook her head in wonder. "I hereby dub you 'Keeper of the Kitchen,'" she proclaimed, tapping me on the shoulder with a spoon.

Astha soon began sluffing off on the job she shared with me: the noon dishes. This meant that when I got to our restaurant almost all the food had been gobbled by swarms of hungry sannyasins, leaving only dahl and scraps of bread. I mentioned it to her and she made excuses. I suggested taking turns: no dice. One day when Vivek brought the thali back and we were alone I told her my problem. Her eyes twinkled.

"I guess you'll have to get that clear with Astha, won't you?" she said lightly and went out, leaving me nonplussed. Wasn't she the boss?

Next day when Astha started to slip out I got between her and the door and told her it was my turn. The sweet smile slipped, her voice came out raspy, angry. "Get out of my way!"

"You can't have your way all the time," I told her in what I hoped was a calm voice. But her face turned red, her fists clenched, her body stiffened. The change was so sudden, from dozy-childish to angry-stubborn-pushy, that I dropped my guard. Astha tried to lunge past me, my fingers tangled in her hair, and then we were on the floor, thrashing about.

I looked up to see Vivek standing in the doorway, laughing. She put the thali down and disappeared. Astha and I did the dishes together in silence. Her pale face was still red and mine felt hot with shame. Such ugly behavior in his kitchen. How could it have happened?

That night Vivek brought me a present from Bhagwan: a backscratcher.

For days I pondered the significance of that backscratcher. Made of bamboo, it had a small design painted on the handle and abstract claws. What could it mean? Were the claws to remind me that I had slipped back into a savage animal past? That I had used violence to remove an itch, when a backscratcher does the same job so gently, so easily? Did the five claws stand for the five senses, a reminder that I should "come to my senses?"

Much later I came to understand that Bhagwan's gifts were just what came to his eye at the moment a person came to his attention; he let existence decide the gift. Sannyasins from all over the world showered presents on him. When he gave them away they all carried the same unspoken message: Look inside. The unconscious mind would throw up whatever meaning the gift had for us.

This fight with Astha sparked a new vision of reality. For me to fight in real life was totally out of character. I couldn't help but see how the raw conflict echoed those in the encounter group. And echoed also the "beatings" Turanti had gone through in Deeksha's kitchen—shocks that each of us came to see as the dynamite that shattered our armor of negativity.

Obviously real-life shocks could give birth to even deeper insights than simulated group conflicts.

It came to me then that the ashram was, in fact, one gigantic encounter group.

Chapter 9

Drunk on Energy

NEERA BOUNCED IN AFTER I'd been working in the kitchen for a month and announced that she was fit to work again. Vivek told her gently that I would be staying on. Neera turned white. She told Vivek I had just nursed Turanti through hepatitis; wasn't that a threat to Bhagwan's health? (I'd told Vivek about it, she had cleared it with Bhagwan.) Vivek simply looked at her, and Neera left the kitchen.

A few months later, as Vivek was stirring the popping mustard seed for the dahl, she asked me casually if I would like to live in Lao Tzu?

Move into the house! My knees wobbled. The idea struck me as delicious, preposterous, hilarious. I knew many of the residents by sight: the two darshan guards—Shiva, a burly red-headed Scot, and Haridas, tall and blonde and Germanic; Teertha, leader of Encounter and his companion Maneesha, editor of the darshan diaries. I cleaned Arup's room, knew she came from a Dutch banking family, but never saw her or Laxmi in the house; they both worked fourteen hour days managing the exploding ashram. Asheesh with his mop of black Italian curls and sly smile I had met; he was in charge of the woodworking shop where Saguna worked. And everyone in the ashram must have known Bhagwan's British physician, Devaraj; dark and handsome, with flashing brown eyes, his great laugh rang out in the cafeteria at lunchtime.

All the live-in staff seemed gloriously ablaze with youth, perhaps half my age. I had turned fifty-six, and the aging showed. I've always been a sun worshipper and my face was wrinkled like the dunes in a desert. The phrase that chuckled through my mind was "Beauties and the Beast!" I don't recall the bite of jealousy, just amazement at my good fortune. I moved in the next day.

I still worked in the kitchen, but now I shared a room with Nirupa, the blonde "goddess" from Toronto who cleaned Bhagwan's room and filled in at many other jobs. Our room wasn't large, but because it was furnished only with two single beds and two dressers it seemed spacious, and big windows made it bright. Nirupa was extremely fastidious. It must have been hard for her to live with someone who stuffed clothes into drawers without folding them and sometimes used the same towel for two days running. But we got along well in our quiet way. We didn't gossip about our work and there wasn't much else to talk about. No newspapers, no radio, no TV.

I spent my evenings dancing in the music group in Buddha Hall, to simple melodies composed and sung by the leader. He looked like a leftover flower child, with long black hair curling over his shoulders and big innocent brown eyes. His songs were innocent, too. I had my favorite:

> *If you don't fight with life*
> *Life simply helps you,*
> *Takes you on its shoulders,*
> *Takes you on its shoulders.*

over a chorus of

> *There is so much magnificence*
> *Near the ocean.*
> *Waves are coming in. . .*
> *Waves are coming in. . .*

Devaraj (George Merideth, M.D., M.B., B.S., M.R.C.P.), Bhagwan's "dark and handsome" doctor.

As we learned the words, the song with its contrapuntal harmony filled the huge space of the hall and poured out to embrace the whole ashram. Sannyasins poured in, joined in. The music built to a wild crescendo. I have always loved to dance alone, and night after night I swirled and spun, twisted and twirled, caught up in the feast of energy.

As months went by, the old hankering to be alone and in touch with the natural world crept up and up. The roof of Lao Tzu House invited with its long expanse of tiny, many-colored tiles, the exotic tropical trees hanging over. The space was used only for drying laundry at one end, it seemed a terrible waste.

Saguna agreed to make me a tiny shelter if I could get him permission to build. I told Vivek of my longing while she was cooking supper for Bhagwan. Next morning she told me Saguna's name had been put on the list of those permitted to enter Lao Tzu; he could start building any time. Speechless with joy and gratitude, I could only look at her.

Saguna built me a tiny fairy-tale shelter in hard, crystal-clear plastic and anchored it solid to the wall. Daytimes I shared the inside room with Nirupa, but nights I spent in this magic space. Moonlight filtered through the trees, monsoon rains exploded on its roof. In storms giant

An evening of ecstatic movement with Bhagwan.

branches crashed on the sides, thunder boomed over and around it, lightning stabbed into it; the wind tried to pick it up and carry it away. In those moments I felt again the bliss of dissolving into a strange, wild universe.

On fine evenings I found a place on the edge of the roof where I could look into the open-sided auditorium and watch the new energy darshans. So many people were swarming into the ashram it was not possible for Bhagwan always to talk to individuals. He began to work with groups, without words. The person receiving darshan he called "a guest in my energy field." He named more than a dozen women as "mediums", calling them his bridges to the guest. One medium knelt behind the guest, another in front, holding his hands.

I knew that life energy is electric, that what moves through my body's nerve cells is the same force that flashes in the sky as lightning. Once I had seen a physics teacher demonstrate an arrangement of coiled wires that could concentrate, intensify and focus an electro-magnetic field. So when Bhagwan arranged his mediums around the guest, I saw him creating a situation in which life energy could move totally.

"Scientists say that we allow only two percent of life to enter, ninety eight percent we keep out," he told us. "And one can live to the maximum! When one-hundred percent of life is allowed to pass through you, then life becomes comprehensible."

Night after night from Lao Tzu roof I watched Bhagwan lead sannyasins into the "peak moments" he had told us about: "when your energy pulsates totally, when you are not holding anything back, when you are drunk, when you are madly drunk—drunk with your own energy, drunk with your own existence."

Bhagwan sits center stage in his small white chair. His guests for energy darshan come forward; he arranges them in specific patterns with the mediums. Dressed alike in plain burgundy robes, the mediums are warm and earthy, like Botticelli women: long-haired, graceful.

Other invited sannyasins sit in rows behind this central group. Light shines on the faces of the nearest, fades away; empty spaces reinforce the contrast of light and dark. The back rows melt into the darkness of the encircling trees.

The lights go out. Music leaps out of the night—crazy, improvised music, starting fast, growing wilder. A flute shrills and drumbeats bounce off the ceiling in a glorious chaos of sound. Humming fills the hall, throbbing, pulsing, expanding. Energy crackles in the air, real as thunder and lightning are real.

Strobe lights flick on, flick off, flick on, flick off. In one vivid flash I glimpse Bhagwan press one thumb to the forehead of a medium, the other to that of a guest. The mediums are a circle of flame around him, dancing, afire with ecstasy; orgasmic.

The music stops. The lights go on.

Bhagwan sits back in his chair. The guests have fallen back into the arms of the mediums. Guards support or carry them to their places. Others come forward. Lights go out, music crashes in.

At the end of the evening, long after Bhagwan has left the auditorium, the cold marble floor of Chuang Tzu is littered with bodies flung about like rag dolls, boneless. Ever so slowly, by ones and twos, the bodies get up and walk the gravel path to Lao Tzu gate, meeting friends and lovers; embracing for long minutes; crying, laughing.

One night I noticed a stormy discontent inside. I was feeling envious. Other people's lives seemed so dramatic. Not just the mediums, all those who had come to darshan over the years; they lived so intensely, pouring out to Bhagwan their great rollercoaster rides: black eyes, breakups, breakthroughs, bliss. If there are no ups and downs, how do I know if I'm progressing?

Awareness of the discontent reminded me of an early darshan when I'd complained about not having any great experiences. I hunted it up in the library. Bhagwan had said, "There is no need. Only fools have great experiences—the very idea of greatness is an ego projection. Be ordinary and you will never be unhappy. People who have great experiences sooner or later fall into the ditch. They have great miseries also. People like Nirgun walk on the balanced ground. They never have peaks, they don't have valleys. So, very good. Just enjoy your silent experience."

Remembering his words left me strangely comforted. I had been looking at these ecstatic people as spiritually more evolved than myself; back to the game of comparing and competing—an old daemon. *I'm not getting A's on my report card!*

In discourse the next day Bhagwan drove home the point that every path is a fiction. We aren't going anywhere, just waking up, waking up and seeing ourselves as we really are: not the image created by our limited senses and conditioned minds, but a creature of pure energy. Just by seeing this reality, we can become detached from our misery without going anywhere, without doing anything.

I was left with a deep sense of wonder: who is this man who has such a profound and tangible effect on those around him?

He is calm, alert, unchanging in changing times and places; and he insists that each one of us has the same ability. It seems a far-off dream to me, and yet he makes it seem so easy, just a flip of the coin away.

On the night of the beating, I realized it wasn't so easy. The moon was full; the light struck each huge brass stud and hinge in the rosewood gates. I'd been for a walk and came in through the gates slowly, anticipating that heavenly peace—and started back in dismay.

The guards were beating a poor Indian, methodically, with sticks. He cried out with each blow. His ragged *dhoti* flapped about his legs.

I rushed forward, then stopped. Laxmi was there, but a Laxmi I'd never seen. She wore a long white night dress, her thick black hair hung down to her waist, her eyes sparked in the light like the brass studs. Her quiet voice was raised, shouting at the guards in Hindi, counting the strokes.

Horror and disbelief flooded my mind; my body froze. How could this be happening? In the ashram of our nonviolent, caring master?

Suddenly I understood. The man's penis was hanging out. Beyond him in the half shadows cowered a young American sannyasin, clutching around her the shreds of her orange robe.

I turned and plunged out the gate, desperate to get away from the crack of the stick, the screams. *Why don't they call the police? How can the ashram countenance such a beating within its gates?*

My feet carried me toward the river, my mind churning. A sixth generation Quaker, raised without punishment, how could I make sense of this? Years with Bhagwan, hearing him talk of reverence for life, and now this?

The path under the trees was dark, I stumbled over tree roots, locked in my fevered thoughts, unaware of my surroundings. *How could he condone such a beating, without a trial, straight out of the dark ages? Does he know about it? But Laxmi is devoted, she would never do anything he wouldn't approve.*

The murmur of rapids sounded through the trees and the darkness lightened as I walked toward the sound. Thoughts still bubbled, but more quietly. Suddenly the memory of a violent act came to me— a hideous act that had to be. Even as a child I knew it.

You have to know how it was. Rover had been my own heart companion for three years. My very own dog, a tan collie with a big white ruff. He ran with me in the morning around the farm to hunt up the cows. He sizzled, a brown streak, up the sandbar to meet me after school. Until one day. . .

The year was 1933, the Great Depression at its worst. Mother had been 'under the weather,' looking pale, crying a lot but never complaining. Father insisted on taking her to Alert Bay to see the doctor, who gave her a tonic and told her she wasn't getting enough protein: she must eat at least two eggs a day. None of us were eating eggs; they were sold to pay for gumboots and sugar and flour.

One morning at breakfast mother had finished eating one egg and started to crack open the second when she burst into tears. "You're all watching me!" she cried, and rushed from the table. And it's true, we were.

The next day Rover didn't come to meet me. Father met me instead, on the path from the house to the barn, just in front of the dairy.

"Have you seen Rover?" I asked him. Only then did I notice his set face. He didn't hug me, didn't touch me, just told me the bitter truth.

"I had to shoot him, Rosemary," he said. "He was eating eggs."

I turned and walked away, walked blindly up the path past the barn, past the Island gardens, out to my haven by the river. But no comfort flowed from the rushing water, from the giant cedars. For hours I lay on the moss floor, my face, my hands, my whole body stiff, unfeeling. No tears came, no anger, no thoughts. Body/heart/mind frozen as ice chunks in the river in winter. Wanting to understand, not understanding. Not knowing what it was that needed understanding.

When I came in late that night, mother caught me to her ferociously, wordlessly, pulled me into the rocking chair by the stove and rocked me like a baby. I broke down then and cried my grief out, my hard lifeless body melting into her soft arms, her tears mingling with mine.

Only an hour, perhaps two, but the bliss of that let go, of touching and being touched, burned into the core of my being.

The memory of Rover lingered as I groped my way out of the dark Indian forest to the river. The path led out into the open riverbed through a grove of silver-barked banyan trees. The long branches fell to the ground, a dense silver circle shimmering in the moonlight. Monsoon rains were long over and the river flowed in a narrow bed, framed with terraces of flat rock and small pools of lavender water hyacinths. I sat on the farthest edge. The river gurgled and danced, mysterious, half dark, half light.

I sat for hours, staring into the swirling water. And it came to me that night that there could never be any one simple answer to a question of right or wrong. Existence itself is mysterious. Where we come from, why we are born, what happens when we die: many questions, no answers. So why should we have opinions about what happens along the way? The river didn't seem to bother. It gurgled and leaped and roared and enjoyed. When it came to rocks it could go around them, over them, or just wash them away. Whatever happened seemed perfectly okay.

I left the river light of heart, freed from the nightmare belief in an absolute right and wrong. Beating the attacker now seemed the only intelligent action. The man's guilt was clear, but the police never acted on ashram complaints; they would have released him. And to let this attempted rape go unpunished would lead to further attacks as surely as Rover would have kept on eating eggs.

In discourse the next morning an American sannyasin wrote of his shock on witnessing the beating. "I felt like leaving the ashram," he wrote. "Bhagwan, did you know about it? I can't believe that you did."

The reply came down with the full force of the master's two-thousand-pound sledgehammer. "Nothing goes on in this ashram that I do not know of," he thundered. "And if you do not like anything that happens here, be on your way. You are wasting your time, and mine."

During the rest of our years in Poona, no further rapes were attempted.

Chapter 10

To Settle is to Become Stuck

THE NEW COMMUNE! We thrilled at the news: Bhagwan's vision for the future had become a pursuit in the present. Our six acres in urban Poona could not contain the vast influx of sannyasins and visitors from every part of the world. Irate neighbors complained to the police daily about our screaming/shouting in the early morning, so the cathartic phase of Dynamic Meditation had to be muted. Newspapers throughout India wrote lurid stories about "the sex guru" and his followers. The climate had become one of open hostility.

Sitting near the front of Buddha Hall as Bhagwan spoke to us one morning in late 1980, I heard a sudden sound overhead and saw a flash of silver falling, clattering on the marble floor in front of the podium: a long, slender knife.

Twenty guards rushed forward, sprang up on the podium and turned to face the crowded hall. They had no weapons, not even sticks, only their bodies to shield Bhagwan from harm. I could see beads of sweat on each flushed forehead. Close behind me I heard other guards take the attacker quietly from the hall. The audience stayed motionless, silent. Bhagwan signalled the guards on the podium to return to their seats, and continued his discourse.

It was clear to all that we needed to move from Poona.

Laxmi, undisputed queen of the ashram, left to prowl the northern states of India for a site. One of her assistants, an intense, unsmiling Indian woman called Sheela, took over her job as Bhagwan's secretary. As Laxmi had done, she came once a day to see him. I sometimes glimpsed her striding down the red corridor, staring straight ahead: intent, one-pointed.

Laxmi found a site for the new commune in Gudjerat, a state in Northern India. Sketches of the proposed housing, designed by a sannyasin architect, were put up in the ashram and offered for sale. Word spread that immense funds would be needed to build the community, and those who had money were asked to buy rooms.

No one asked me for money, but I'd never paid for my room in Jesus House and now the time seemed right. My house in Vancouver had been sold, the money was in the bank there. I signed up to buy a three-bedroom condominium, feeling elated. This time I'd be prepared for family visits.

Time sagged as we waited, eager for news of our home-to-be. Answering a question about it, Bhagwan asked why we were so impatient? We must surely know that we would just get settled in our new commune and he would toss it in the air.

We never did get settled. The dream community in North India evaporated. There was much good-natured grumbling, but no money had been paid, only our dreams had been shattered. And we all knew that shattering dreams was Bhagwan's chief delight.

Suddenly it was announced that we were going to move to Saswad, a farming area twenty miles from Poona. Saguna was co-opted by Richard, the construction foreman, to help build the new commune. He and dozens of other workers took turns coming to the ashram for morning satsang. Laxmi remained in North India; rumor had it that she was not happy with Saswad and was determined to find a bigger and better site.

While Saguna was in Saswad, my eldest son Craig wired: Glen had died of a heart attack. I felt no regret, no grief—as if my marriage to him, loaded with love and jealousy, had happened to someone else. My thoughts of him were fond; that was all.

This lack of response disturbed me. Was I becoming callous, to be so unmoved by his death? My daily life had acquired a certain detachment: aggressive rickshaw drivers didn't intimidate me anymore, a pilfered purse seemed a natural event. But this was something else. I saw that I had begun to look on death itself as a natural event.

Bhagwan often spoke of death as part of life, a door opening on the unknown. He scoffed at our seriousness, our taboos, and told the most outrageous jokes. Sending word of his dad's death to Saguna, I was tempted to use one.

A college student phones home and asks his brother Blake for news.

"Well, David, your cat is dead," Blake tells him.

David falls apart and cries uncontrollably.

"Damn it, Blake," he yells. "You know how I loved that cat. You should have broken it to me gently. You could have said, 'Dave, the other day your cat climbed out the window. Then it crawled up the rainspout and got out on the roof. It slipped and fell,' and then you could have told me it died."

"Dave, I'm really sorry," apologizes Blake.

"Okay, forget it," says David. "How's Mom?"

"Well, David, last night Mom climbed out the window. Then she crawled up the rainspout and got out on the roof. . . ."

I started to write, "Beloved Saguna, yesterday Glen climbed out the window." Then I tore it up and wrote it straight. Dying still wasn't something to joke about.

In May of 1981 it was announced that Bhagwan had developed severe back pain; a specialist from England confirmed Devaraj's diagnosis of disc disease. Bhagwan would no longer speak to us each morning. Instead, he would sit with us in Buddha Hall in satsang, a spiritual practice where disciples commune with the master without words, against a background of soft, exquisite music.

The announcement stunned me. For nearly seven years Bhagwan's spicy discourses had started my days with laughter, and I wanted more. But he had warned us that in the new commune he would withdraw from us physically in order to be more accessible spiritually.

The period of silence he now entered would continue for three and a half years. During this time he gave no discourses, no darshans;

he spoke only as needed, to Vivek, to Sheela, and to his medical staff, and on rare occasions, to other individuals.

From his very first public appearance after resigning his professorship in Jabalpur University, Bhagwan had pointed the way toward silence: "a silence shimmering with joy and delight, a silence dancing in mirth and merriment; silence without, and the energy dancing within."

"It is only man who creates noise," he told an early meditation camp in Mt. Abu. "These birds, they sing silence. These rivers rushing toward the ocean, they sing silence. It is man who has brought word into existence, and through words he has become lost in the jungle of language."

In childhood I had known the joy of silent communing with nature. In two years of silence here in the ashram I had become aware of many hidden facets of my own nature. But it seemed to me that I had also missed much. One day after a discourse on Buddha, I sent in a question/poem:

Bhagwan,
    What is the key to this puzzle?
    The Buddha says, Speak less. And silence is beautiful,
    For what have I to say?
    Tales of the past, dreams of the future
    Giddy gossip or reasoned argument
    All
    Taste phony to the tongue.
    Silence is beautiful, and yet
    The sound of merry chatter over teacups
    Echoes the carefree chirping of the birds
    Energy flowing in a joyous cosmos. Bhagwan, tell me
    What is the key to this puzzle?

Bhagwan answered next morning in discourse.

"Nirgun, the more you enjoy gossiping, the deeper will be your silence. These are polar opposites and they balance each other. If you work hard during the day, you will sleep a deep sleep in the night.

"Life functions through the polar opposites. The chirping of the birds is beautiful—but have you watched that when it suddenly stops there is a great silence? The silence is deepened by the song of the birds. The silence that follows the storm is the deepest, the most profound.

"If you cut out all your gossiping, all your talking, your silence will be superficial, your silence will be a kind of sadness. It will not have depth. From where will it get depth? It can get depth only from its polar opposite.

"If you want to really rest, first dance—dance to abandon. Let every fibre of your body and being dance, and then follows a relaxation, a rest which is total. You need not do it, it happens on its own.

"Take life very playfully. Then you can have both worlds together. This world and that, sound and silence; love and meditation; being with people, relating, and being alone."

Now in satsang the wild wordless music of flute, sitar and drums soared and throbbed in the silence, enticing, evocative, bringing to vivid life the magic spaces of my childhood: the lapping waves, the wind-stirred leaves, the bird song; the melting. And now, here was the bustling cafeteria, the chatter, the laughter, the hugs—a different melting. The dance of opposites.

Change shimmered in the very air of the ashram. Outside specialists came into Lao Tzu to confer with Devaraj about Bhagwan. Vivek's time went into caring for his health, and Pragya took over cooking for him. One of his earliest Indian disciples, she was ecstatic to be in his kitchen. I loved to watch her hands as she cleaned dahl and rolled chapatis with the lightning skill of a sleight-of-hand artist.

One evening when I was alone in the kitchen Vivek came in.

"Nirgun," she said quietly, "we're going to America. You and Pragya will need to pack four meals for Bhagwan. You're coming with us on the plane."

"When do we leave?" I asked, as calmly as if she'd asked me to make her favorite snack, fried cheese/bread triangles.

"Soon. We won't know till the last minute," she answered. "And Nirgun," she put her hand lightly on my shoulder, "it's imperative for Bhagwan's safety that you don't tell *anybody*."

"Not even Saguna?" The words tumbled out. Vivek answered with her silence.

"Of course not," I added quickly. "Not even Saguna."

She hugged me then, the first time ever. I remembered that hug every time I saw Saguna and choked back my longing to tell him.

That we were going to America didn't surprise me. If Bhagwan were to need an operation on his back, it could be more safely done in the West. I thought he would fit with America. His ideas were so fresh, so young, so avant garde: all the traits Americans cherish. And America itself is so young, so receptive to new technology and new ideas.

Prophecy never has been my strong suit.

On May 31, 1981 I stood on Lao Tzu porch for the last time and namasted Bhagwan as he stepped into the white armor-plated Rolls. The house and garden staff, choking back their tears, gathered to see him go.

Pragya, Chetana and I scrambled into the second car and followed the Rolls through Lao Tzu gate. The secret had been well-kept; we edged our way on the crowded road of the ashram to the front gate, and no one noticed that Bhagwan was leaving.

On the road to Bombay our driver braked abruptly. The Rolls had pulled to the side of the road. Bhagwan, holding Vivek's arm, was strolling across the green verge. Cars were stopping: in his white robe and knitted cap Bhagwan was instantly recognizable. Our secrecy was blown.

"Whatever are they doing!" I exclaimed to Pragya. She grinned at me. When I looked again, Bhagwan was nonchalantly squatting in the traditional Indian posture. Peeing.

We stopped at a disciple's home in Bombay while he rested and ate. Late that night we drove to the airport and boarded a Pan Am 747 jumbo jet, flight #001, bound for New York.

The entire first class section had been reserved for Bhagwan, Vivek and Devaraj, together with Nirupa as cleaner and Pragya and I as cooks, with full use of its galley. Pragya and I stowed away the food we had brought in the bright shining fridge, and served up his lunch smack on time, at 11 o'clock.

Sheela brought up a bottle of champagne and persuaded Bhagwan to hold a glass as a joke while she poured and our photographer took a picture.

"That'll shatter a few expectations!" I whispered to Pragya.

A sense of delicious absurdity kept me on the point of giggling:

that I, a nature child from the back of beyond, should be washing a sterling silver thali and fine china in the galley of a jumbo jet hurtling along at four hundred miles per hour, six miles above the Atlantic Ocean.

After the meal I rubbed his thali till it shone—kept on rubbing in an excess of high spirits and then gave Pragya a great hug.

"We're going to live in America!" I laughed. "No more beggars in the streets, no more horrid smells, no more fanatics attacking us. You're going to love it!"

Like I said, prophecy has never been my thing.

The noisy snarl of New York traffic surpassed the Poona chaos of sacred cows and honking rickshaws and felt more dangerous because of the speed. And the *smell!* The air stank of car exhaust; felt gritty in my eyes, on my skin. The dark and bland colors of people's clothes depressed me. I recalled my joy and relief seven years earlier when my black pants gave way to sunshine colors. Now we had stepped backward, from the full glory of technicolor into a black and white film.

On the way to New Jersey the streets were empty of people: just long rows of buildings and automobiles, no sign of life anywhere. Compared to the teeming, lively crowds of India, America seemed a graveyard, the people already encapsulated in a shrine of house or car.

Chetana had the same reaction. "I looked at the deserted streets and for a moment I panicked," she told me later. "I thought maybe there had been a nuclear explosion and everyone was dead."

At the end of a winding road that passed briefly through a forest, poised at the top of a small hill there sat a replica of a medieval castle, complete with tower, round leaded windows with stained glass, and heavy scrolled doors.

Pragya and I ensconced ourselves in the second story kitchen. I was given a tiny room on the same floor. I loved taking the dish towels up the winding steps of the turret and hanging them out to dry in a space that looked out over the famous skyline of Manhattan.

Vivek brought word that Bhagwan wanted to try American food. For two weeks we experimented. I invented a vegetarian shepherd's pie and Asheesh came in to cook an omelette and to make spaghetti, which Bhagwan rejected because it looked like Indian worms. Dry cereal, commercial yogurt, breads, pastries, soft drinks—the only ones to stick were Diet Coke and Perrier water. We went back to the basics: dahl, veggies, chapatis, curd, chutney, fruit.

Still keeping the warm hues of the sun we dropped the loose- fitting Poona robes and wore Western-style clothes. Chetana looked like something out of Vogue in a fitted magenta jumpsuit with dozens of zippered pockets. I chose a soft deep red pant suit.

One day Bhagwan came down the stairs to inspect a new arrival: a black and silver convertible Rolls Royce, the first of a fleet that Bhagwan's many rich followers were to shower on him. We gathered on the lawn to watch his response. To our amazement he got in the driver's seat and started off down the hill, trying out all the buttons as he went. Windows rolled open and shut, the hood went up and down. As he drove out of sight I rolled on the grass in a rush of fearful delight, knowing he hadn't driven a car for twenty years, and then in India, on the "wrong" side of the road.

Bhagwan began to go for a drive every day. Soon he invited us, one by one, to accompany him. Vivek went with him each time, returning white and shaking; sometimes she tossed down a glass of whiskey to calm her nerves.

"He drives fast!" Chetana told us. "He says there is too much fear in the car."

If people couldn't relax, Bhagwan said, he would stop driving altogether. My turn came on a day of heavy rain.

I sit beside Vivek in the back of a pale blue Rolls Royce and sink into the luxury seat, full of delight just to be here. Bhagwan sits totally still and silent behind the wheel. He eases the car into motion with rapt attention.

The car picks up speed. We sweep around corners onto the turnpike. Traffic thunders down the highway, going fast—but we are going faster. Changing lanes, weaving in and out as tiny openings appear, slipping for a nanosecond on the wet road, we ride the waves of traffic.

Watching oncoming cars bear down, feeling the car twist and slide past at the last second, I live again a moment of the past: uprooted snags roaring towards me in a raging yellow current, the sharp thrust of my paddle. The same mad exhilaration grips me. I am totally alive, afire with energy on this wild, wild ride.

Heavy rain blurs our vision between each sweep of the wipers. Vivek is white. Her fingers dig into my arm. She starts to cry out but chokes it back.

I put my arm around her, hug her silently. Reminding her without words that we are with a master—fully conscious, master of himself; master of the car he drives.

When Vivek brought back the supper dishes she looked at me strangely. "Bhagwan asked me to tell you," she said, "that you are the only one so far who has been present in the car."

Supervised by Deeksha, Richard and his building crew from Poona worked day and night to reconstruct the castle on orders from Sheela. They tore out walls, solid mahogany doors and leaded glass windows, turning the castle into a modern anonymous dwelling. We all hated it. But I recalled the E. J. Gold workshop in California, painting white latex over rosewood walls. Was this the same lesson, no attachment to ideas of how things should be?

The construction workers toiled day and night. Their Indian tan disappeared, their faces became thinner. I wondered why more workers weren't brought in. *Why not bring Saguna? He'd love to come and work on the castle.*

The question niggled till I finally put it to Richard. He laughed, bitterly. "I've asked three times," he said. "We all want him here. He's a great worker and easy to be around. Sheela just says no."

Astonished, I asked, "Why would Sheela nix Saguna? She doesn't even know him!"

Richard looked around, then answered in a low voice. "Because he's your son, Nirgun. Sheela *hates* anyone from LaoTzu."

He walked away, putting an end to further talk. Leaving me confused and alarmed. He was Vivek's lover now, he wouldn't speak lightly. But why should Sheela hate LaoTzu people?

Events left me little time to brood over her hatred. As news of Bhagwan's whereabouts spread, sannyasins poured in without invitation, crowding the small town of Montclair, highly visible in their red clothes. A Christian fanatic from Germany came too, spreading false, ugly stories about Bhagwan and our commune in India. Hooligans spraypainted "Go Home" on the walls of the castle, exploded loud mock bombs, shattered windows.

Bhagwan as automobile afficionado.

We needed to find land for the new commune *now.* Vivek and Richard didn't trust Sheela's ability to find it. A land developer before he took sannyas, Richard used his contacts. One day he exploded into the kitchen, his blue eyes bright with excitement.

"Where's Vivek?" he demanded, and I pointed toward her room. As he plunged through the door he waved a sheaf of papers at me.

"I've found it, Nirgun!" he whisper/shouted.

Vivek showed me the brochures after he left. More than a hundred acres in New Mexico, on the banks of a large river; irrigated, lush green fields, orchards; more land available, relaxed zoning. We danced around the kitchen, sure that Richard had found our Shangri La.

But when she brought back the supper dishes, Vivek looked dispirited. Bhagwan had rejected the New Mexico paradise.

A few days later she came into the kitchen with a forced grin on her face. "Guess what, Nirgun!" she exclaimed, laughing bitterly. "Sheela has found a place. We're going to Oregon. To the desert!"

Chapter 11

Of Hamburgers and Heaven

I HATED IT before I saw it.

From the time we turned off the main highway on the road to Rancho Rajneesh, my heart plummeted in slow motion. The ride seemed a descent into disaster. Sagebrush and stunted juniper lined endless curves that dropped through bare hills, gullies and dry creek beds. A thick blanket of dust swirled out from the wheels, swirled back through the windows as we drove the county road, forever and forever winding.

It was late summer, 1981. Pragya and I were being driven from the Portland airport to the new commune, to prepare Bhagwan's kitchen for his arrival the next day.

The car turned the thousandth corner and breath rushed in through my open mouth. "This is the ranch," said our sannyasin driver. He pulled off on a huge rock outcrop jutting over a great emptiness.

Wordless, I got out of the car, stood on the brink and stared. Spread out before me in unbelievable immensity lay a river valley. I stared at the low rolling hills, hills rolling into one another like waves on the ocean, as far as the eye could see. The sun had set but the orange glow lingered in the sky; the hills were bathed in purple haze. For long minutes I stood, drinking in the *vastness* of that space, no sign of human hand save the small winding road.

Bhagwan often chided us with a chuckle, "You've got eternity!" And in that moment, in that flowing, open space, I knew what he meant.

We drove the rest of the way in silence, past sandy slopes and red rocks carved into silent statues by the wind. In contrast to the soft, lush, changing vegetation of the Pacific coast, the country here was an austere Zen creation with a waiting, ageless beauty.

We turned off the main road and a few minutes later crossed a makeshift bridge over a meandering muddy creek. The car pulled to a stop beside two trailers set at right angles to one another in a sage-brush and juniper canyon. I stepped out into a whirlwind of light and motion.

The hillside was lit with huge floodlamps. Sannyasins in red bib overalls and brown gumboots scrambled back and forth scrubbing the trailer stairs, painting trim, polishing windows. A backhoe ran back and forth through them, leveling the driveway. A dozen red-clad bodies carried squares of green turf from a huge pile, laid them with care, making a lawn in front of the trailer. In the midst of them I glimpsed blond, blue-eyed Richard orchestrating: calm at the centre of the cyclone.

Tools clattered to the ground as they saw us. I recognized many old friends from the ashram—Turanti! Her red hair flamed like a homing beacon. She was here, on the ranch, I didn't know! I leaped out of the car and hugged her. When Bhagwan left Poona in June she'd gone home to Vancouver, expecting to be called to the Castle, and instead had been asked to go direct to the ranch in Oregon.

We took a long, noisy tea break while these earliest pioneers erupted with exuberant horror stories: handpicking tons of rock from the fertile fields on the river, junking out tons of rusted cars and cans and wire; plowing thickets of weeds into hardpan soil, planting 150 acres of sunflowers "because they grow faster than weeds—and all those bright flowers dancing in the wind!"

Richard had to shout over the hubbub to get us back to work.
I followed Pragya inside to make the kitchen squeaky clean, stopping
once to look back at the mad scramble of red-clad bodies. I had to
laugh, thinking how impossible it would be to explain to an outsider.
It looked for all the world like the activity of ants, or of bees preparing
a hive for the queen. But this was no blind act of nature. The emerald
grass spread outward from the trailers, twinkling magic in the flood
lights, adding beauty to nature's bare-bones effort in a fully conscious
act, born of love.

One of the trailers was for the staff, one for Bhagwan; they had
been connected by a long corridor. The kitchen was the link between
the staff trailer and Bhagwan's trailer. Its beige linoleum and ersatz
wood walls were cheap and ugly, but the sweeping view from the big
kitchen windows—open space with the creek running through and
distant craggy bluffs—restored my spirits.

The trailer had six bedrooms, a living room, mudroom, bathroom
and laundry. I took a small room adjoining the kitchen, Pragya chose
one off the living room. We cleaned and polished till the small hours
of the morning.

The sun is low in the sky next day when a tiny twister of dust
erupts on the farthest stretch of the county road, and a cry goes up:
"He's coming!" I squeeze into the swarm of workers on the new lawn,
our bright reds a curving border of welcome framing the vivid green.
We are dewy-clean and quiet, showing no sign of last night's chaos.

The swirl of dust comes fast around the curves. Music from guitars and flutes wafts into the desert to welcome Bhagwan. Many of the
sannyasins here have not seen him for months. They laugh and cry
quietly.

A long grey limousine winds up the driveway and stops. Bhagwan
steps out onto the new lawn, smiling, a roguish here-we-go-again smile.
I see, close-up, the long fingers of his hands coming together, his eyes
slowly moving over the silent sannyasins. For an instant they look
directly into mine. Gratitude overwhelms me—that he is here, that I
am here.

So began for me the saga of Rancho Rajneesh, a story of long labor
and light laughter, of deception and delight, of worship and war; of

absolute power and its bitter dregs. Life, encapsulated.

I loved the ranch, every bit of it. Silence hung in the air like a scentless, mysterious perfume. Under that vast open sky with its feeling of limitless space, of freedom to roam the earth unchecked, unhindered, the old magic of my childhood came back to me. . . .

> I turned the curve in the path to the river, and stopped. My heart stopped too. The big red canoe that we all paddled to school floated there as always, moored to the log landing by a thick rope. Tied to the log was a second, smaller canoe, only eight feet long, unpainted, chipped out of a cedar log—a native dugout. A red cedar paddle slanted across the seat.
>
> I moved slowly down the hill, reading the cardboard sign printed in BIG letters from bow to stern: *To Rosemary, on the Occasion of her Tenth Birthday.*
>
> I untied the canoe slowly, stepped in, picked up the paddle. Even before I started to stroke my fingers were warming, the wind felt less cold. I drifted and paddled, paddled and drifted; getting the feel of the tiny craft, going with the current, destination unknown. My spirits soared with each passing minute. Not the pleasure of possession, what flooded through me was the joy of freedom: freedom to roam, to delight in the rippling water, the play of sun and shadows, the sudden squalls—on my very own.

Bhagwan said to me once in a Poona darshan, "There is no need for great experiences. Just taking a shower and you feel peaceful; working in the garden, and suddenly the clouds disperse and the sun has come and one feels good. Just sitting doing nothing and one is in this moment here-now. One is in heaven and paradise has happened. Real spiritual experiences are these, very ordinary."

The new Lao Tzu kitchen was a very ordinary unit of a very ordinary cheap trailer: long plastic counters, brown plastic cupboards, cheap steel sink, linoleum floor.

My job was commonplace too. Wash the dahl: select and prepare the veggies for Pragya to cook for Bhagwan's lunch at eleven, dice fruit, make juice, cook lunch for Vivek, wash dishes, clean kitchen; break; repeat above for supper at six. In almost total silence. We didn't gossip in the kitchen.

Routine, ordinary. An extraordinary ordinariness.

The first day in that kitchen burned into my memory. Red-cheeked in the frosty air, glowing with delight at being here in Lao Tzu, the gardeners hurried up the curving driveway, their wicker baskets brimming with vegetables: tiny carrots, scrubbed to shine like jewels, dainty spinach leaves and dark green broccoli; light green cabbage, new lettuce, and tiny peas; delicate butterfly squash and bindi. The cornucopia was laced with fine sprays of meti and coriander, sparked with a dash of radish. So radiant and fresh was every leaf, so infectious the joy of the bearers, I spread their offering on the counter reverently. We hugged without words.

The heaping colorful baskets inspired me to brighten the dull kitchen counters with eight great square glass bottles filled with every color of lentils, from the green of split peas to the pinkish-grey of urad dahl and the bright orange of masoor dahl.

Intrigued by the popping mustard seeds, the sweet/sharp scent of frying coriander and cumin, I learned from Pragya how to make dahl and then went on to create an East/West hybrid, a dahl "hamburger:" lentils cooked to thick mush, spiced, shaped into round patties and fried in butter. Vivek loved them, and so did Bhagwan when she gave him a bite.

On such a humble hub does the wheel of existence turn. One day in the winter of that first year, Vivek sat me down alone at the kitchen table, her face serious. "Nirgun," she said, "Pragya is unhappy on the ranch. She's going back to India tomorrow."

I stared at her. Pragya had told me she hated Sheela and missed her friends. But she had been with Bhagwan for so many years!

"Who will cook now?" I asked. Indian Mukti and her cousin, both of whom had cooked for Bhagwan in the early days, were on the ranch.

Vivek's face lit up with a great grin. "Bhagwan wants *you* to cook for him," she said happily. "He really likes your dahl burgers."

Delight flooded my veins, then mixed with horror as her words sank in. Cook for Bhagwan? The greatest honor, and a huge responsibility. No more slightly scorched patties; veggies must be cooked *but still crisp*; and what about the. . . .

"Chapatis?" The word came out as a croak. "Me, make chapatis?"

Vivek laughed. "He's going to have toast instead, with no butter," she told me. "Devaraj thinks losing weight will help his back."

The next day I made coriander chutney and mung dahlburgers, steamed the veggies, prepared his round silver thali. Three delicate bowls brimmed with tiny orange carrots, red beets, and dark green spinach. A fourth held the bright green chutney, a fifth, white yogurt. A small china plate held the dahl patty; another cradled two pieces of toasted ranch bread. A tall cutglass tumbler of pink fruit juice, a silver bowl with a jumble of fresh fruit. On a soft folded napkin, a small gold spoon and a tiny toothpick.

I felt like Grandma Moses must have when she finished her first painting. When she brought back the empty thali Vivek gave me a thumbs up, and I'd just won the four-minute mile.

Bhagwan's widowed mother lived on the ranch, a tiny woman who spoke no English. When she came to visit her son in Lao Tzu, she would always stop off in the kitchen on the way to his room, greeting me with a wordless namaste; checking the pans and pots on the stove to see what was cooking, giving me a huge smile and a bashful hug.

For three years a feeling of delighted absurdity stayed with me: that I, a fricassee-chicken-and-apple-pie Canadian cook, should be serving such a simple meal to a man who could order up any delicacy in the world.

The simple meals became even simpler. Bhagwan's doctor, Devaraj, came to the kitchen with scales and meticulous directions to weigh every carrot, every pea, every ounce of fruit juice. Under our tender care Bhagwan lost weight, and more weight, and still more. My life centered on the act of cooking and cleaning up. The same routine, the same food, twice a day, every day.

I am preparing Bhagwan's supper in late afternoon. The sun floods over my hands as I wash orange lentils in the sink. Outside the window a peacock is preening, pure white against green bushes. Poplars hiss as they bend in the desert wind.

A deep silence fills the kitchen. As I watch the clear water swirl over the bright lentils, silence washes over me too.

I turn at a hint of movement. Bhagwan is standing in the doorway, smiling, namasteing. Looking at me, saying in his oh-so-soft voice, "Hello, Nirgun."

He has never come through the kitchen before, nor will he come again. His presence is so vivid I stand wordless, palms together in greeting as he passes through to the staff trailer, then passes back again to his own trailer down the corridor. A few seconds? minutes? and for what? I don't know, and it doesn't matter.

My role as Bhagwan's cook thrust me into the top ranks of the commune's "spiritual elite." I kept to myself the secret of my success: the dahlburger.

Only one cloud came to interfere with this simple idyll, but that cloud was heavy, dark. My son Blair wrote, and through his distraught words I glimpsed his terrible grief. His marriage had broken up, his wife had been given custody of their two children, Kelly and Nancy. He'd been told to apply for visiting privileges. But he didn't want visiting privileges. He wanted his kids. Come up and help!

My heart turned to stone as I read. The children had been the centre of his life, how could he stand the shock of losing them? But I knew that, unless evidence of her total unfitness is given, the mother of young children is always awarded custody. Nothing I could do or say, no lawyer's magic tongue, could alter that fact. And to be pulled between two warring parents would guarantee a hellish life for the kids.

Every fiber of my mother-heart longed to jump on the first bus out, just to be with Blair—even knowing I could not help, even knowing that to leave could close the door of Lao Tzu to me, just as 4 years before it had been closed to Neera and I had taken her place.

But then the Biblical story of one of Christ's disciples came back to me, when Christ reprimands him for wanting to turn back to meet family responsibilities. I puzzled and wept far into the night.

The next morning I woke with a crystal-clear answer: *Blair can come to the ranch! The comradeship, the peace, the hard work, the music will help to heal the terrible wound.* Breathing a silent prayer of gratitude that the commune had insisted I keep a few hundred dollars for my own use, I wrote Blair, enclosing the bus fare; waited in trembling hope for him to appear.

Ten days later I tore open a return letter. The 100 dollar bill fell out. There was no message.

It was the darkest moment of my life.

I threw myself into building the new commune, working night after night till I fell exhausted into bed.

In Poona Bhagwan had told me to let work be my meditation; in Oregon from 1981 to 1985 it became everyone's meditation. Months were to flow into years as we blistered our way through the barren rocky hills, throwing up dams, bridges, cluster housing, huge cafeterias, workshops, airport, hospital, shops, a university, a crematorium— the air electric with energy that poured into work by day and discoing by night.

But as we threw ourselves into the task of pioneering, not one of us saw the danger that we would forget the reason we came to Bhagwan. We had come to pour our energy inward, to search out the unconscious emotions and drives that so often played havoc with our lives. Now, instead, we were focussing outward, on the commune.

Bhagwan remained in silence. Sheela had full charge of ranch affairs, reporting to him daily. Later he told us he had offered her a room in LaoTzu, but she chose to live apart with her staff of "moms." His only visitor, she came unfailingly each evening to see him, unless she was away from the ranch on business.

Only once in our four years on the ranch was her talk almost cancelled. In early December of that first year the heaviest rain in decades flooded down from the grey skies and Muddy Creek rose six feet, thick with mud pouring down from the stripped hills.

The footbridge washed out first. The rushing waters hurled debris against our new-built dams. All three broke overnight, leaving a yellow torrent thirty feet wide rushing between Lao Tzu and the rest of the commune. Weeks of strenuous work were wiped out. The heavy rains made repair impossible, and ranch workers relaxed in the heavenly bliss of their first holiday.

One vivid picture of that flood stays with me: Sheela crossing the swollen river to keep her daily appointment with Bhagwan. Dark eyes blazing, long black hair streaming in the cold rain and wind, she forced a terrified, snorting black stallion through the yellow surging water— matching his brute power with her own, and winning.

It was my first clear glimpse of why Sheela had been chosen to carve a city out of a wilderness.

Chapter 12

Pioneers on the Big Muddy

ROM DAY ONE on the ranch Sheela cut herself off from the rest of the commune. She set up her headquarters, called Jesus Grove, in a canyon a mile away from Lao Tzu. Along with her aides, called "moms," she held court in a newly renovated house, awash in Western luxury: shag rugs, swank furniture, a bar in the vestibule laden with fruit juices and enormous chocolate chip cookies. Meals boasting Western delicacies were served in her huge private dining room. The stylish furnishings and food were said to be needed to impress visiting dignitaries. But Sheela and her moms took root there, slept, worked and ate there in superlative style. Workers crowded into the old farm house to sleep.

Sannyasins all over the world were pouring in money to build the new commune in America. Thousands longed to come, but no housing for them existed. Sheela's office decided who could come to the ranch.

Meanwhile eating conditions for workers were savagely primitive. With winter upon us we still ate outside, hands turning blue and numb, at tables clustered on a bare space near the farmhouse. By lunchtime each day the mud had thawed and the table legs sank in, leaving the tops wildly aslant. By supper time they were frozen solid again and we had to hold onto plates and cups to keep them from sliding off.

Turanti worked in the tiny farmhouse kitchen, cranking out meals for the hungry hordes. This kitchen lay within sight of the swank and privilege of Jesus Grove, and one day after lunch she exploded.

"There's no one to wash the clothes, just whoever in the kitchen has a minute free," she fumed. "I'm in the laundry this morning, the room is jam-packed from floor to ceiling with dirty work pants and flannel shirts and wool socks and sheets and pillow cases and towels and these bulky jackets.

"So I'm stuffing the washer full and I see this incredibly fine white damask tablecloth on the shelf." The words poured out of her, her brown eyes shooting sparks. "An *enormous* tablecloth. It's got a note attached '**Iron Perfectly for Jesus Grove**.'" Turanti stopped and stared venomously down the road that led to the luxury dwelling. "How come Sheela has damask on her table, and we have ice on ours?"

"Isn't it just another of those games people play around Bhagwan?" I asked her. "What's the difference between Sheela and Deeksha? Sheela put Shiva in a laboring job, after he'd been a guard at darshan for years, and he left the ranch. Deeksha did the same kind of thing to you in Poona and you accepted it. You knew Bhagwan was just using her as his Zen stick. She had her own private stash of goodies, her own special friends she invited for meals, remember? And what about the time she dumped her chai on the floor in front of you and said, 'Clean it up?'"

But Turanti insisted that was somehow different. "Deeksha was Italian," she said, as if that explained everything. "She had feelings, she was in her heart. She looked right at me when she did it, and I knew she saw the hairball of anger I'm always choking on; she was trying to get me to spit it out. She played with me to shock me out of it. Sheela is just plain power-hungry."

Turanti was right, but I didn't know it then. Not even when I had my own encounter with Sheela.

After Bhagwan left Poona, western sannyasins vacated the ashram, leaving a handful of Indian sannyasins to maintain the property. Saguna went to Vancouver, expecting to be called to the ranch to help with construction. Three months later he wrote me that he still hadn't been called and he *really* wanted to come; could I do anything?

I went to see Dolma, one of Sheela's moms. Dolma hailed from Vancouver and I felt connected to her. She told me about a new program of short-term visits for those who had their own van or truck to sleep in.

I phoned Saguna that night. His wild excitement came over the wires. He'd borrow a friend's truck and come first thing in the morning!

The next day I was called to Dolma's office.

"Sheela says Saguna is not to come," she told me.

"But he's already left!" I gasped, stunned by this sudden reversal.

"He won't be allowed on the ranch under any circumstances," Dolma insisted. She didn't meet my eyes.

Richard's whisper came back to me: "Sheela *hates* anyone from Lao Tzu!"

I wrote to Sheela, explaining my actions in detail. Not trusting her now, I kept a copy of the letter.

Saguna phoned from our newly-purchased hotel in Portland.

"The guys on duty here tell me I won't be allowed on the ranch. They are amazed, they all know me. But they've had orders direct from Sheela."

I talked to Vivek then, gave her the copy of my letter; she took it straight to Bhagwan. Sheela had told him I was trying to smuggle Saguna onto the ranch!

It was my word against Sheela's. Bhagwan did what he always told us to do: check out the facts, find the truth. He sent to Sheela's office to get a copy of my letter. Then Vivek sat at the kitchen table and matched the two, word for word. My heart filled with awe and delight: that he should treat with such care such a small matter when it came to his notice.

That night Vivek brought me Bhagwan's message: "Saguna can come *and stay forever.*" She added, with a conspiratorial grin, "He gave Sheela what-for for lying to him."

Next day Saguna and I fell into each other's arms. He was blown away by the hair's breadth escape: permanent exile from his home and friends. "Not just friends you have a beer with on Saturday nights," he told me, laughing through his tears. "These are friends you can cry with, pour your heart out to, any time, any place."

Saguna was put to work on the construction crew as Richard and his hustling hundred built Magdalena, our huge communal cafeteria, in just two months. His job sounded safe till I came by one afternoon to watch him at work.

They'd just had a cement pour and orchestrated panic filled the air. Speed was the name of the game, the concrete set fast. A dozen men and women worked like a chorus line, raking the huge mound of grey guck over a hundred foot strip; another lot followed with scrapers on four-foot handles. Behind them a single individual with a bullfloat—a very long paddle—flattened the lumps like icing on a cake, and one more wielded a gadget that looked like an upside-down helicopter.

They all had the flushed, lively look of kids at play. Laughing, talking to each other in phony cowboy accents piled onto English already heavy with other speech patterns. I recognized German, Spanish and French just in the snatches I could hear over the roar of trucks and the machine-gun rattle of bolts being tightened.

I couldn't see Saguna at first, till a clatter far down the building caught my attention. I looked up—and broke out in a freezing sweat. He was balanced on a tiny beam of steel that stretched the full width of the giant building, thirty feet above the ground, carrying one end of a steel brace; across a twenty foot gap, his partner in insanity carried the other end. They set it in place, then ran back for another from a pile at the end of the steel ribbon. No safety harness, no safety net.

I'd pioneered from scratch before, but the orchestrated scene before me bore no resemblance to my ox-and-canoe childhood. As I watched the frolicsome daring of my son building this shelter in the middle of nowhere, memories flooded back. . . .

I'd follow Dad when he went to fell trees for firewood, running to keep up to his long steps. I can still see him cutting into a giant cedar, tall and dark in his navy blue turtleneck and black jeans, the bright chips flying, the sweat pouring down his lean brown face; still hear the ring of his shout, "Timber-r-r-r!" and the rush of the great tree as it fell.

My father was a fifth generation Quaker, my mother a Method-ist. They didn't preach, but they did welcome all comers, from home-sick fishermen to the Archbishop du Pencier, to home-cooked meals spiced with great conversation and uproarious laughter. Dad radi-ated enthusiasm for life. Coming back upriver after a few days on his fishwarden job he'd tie down the rudder on his thirty-foot gasboat and climb the mast to holler "Tea!" as he went by the house. He was a teetotaller in a land of hard-drinking loggers and fishermen, but never a killjoy. Once a logger summed up his irrepressible high spirits: "Lawrie is the only man I know who can get drunk on tea."

He hadn't always been so laid back. I loved the old pictures of him, in funny-looking pants on a shiny horse or camera-stiff in a starched shirt with a stand-up collar, a university dandy in upper-middle-class Bristol.

At age eighteen he took off for the farthest point in the British Empire and homesteaded four hundred acres of land in remote Kingcome Inlet. Rich delta land, a virgin-forest mountainside, a sturdy four-bedroom house, a logging camp across the river to take all he could produce. Two years after he brought home a bride the sturdy home burned to the ground.

When I came along ten years later ten of us were living in a rough fourteen-by-twenty shack; the barn, as any farmer's wife will swear to on a Bible wet with tears, has to come first. Working on his own, a raw Englishman with only hammer, axe and crosscut, it had taken dad years to put together the huge building. He laid it all out on the ground, complete with pulleys; then the loggers came over from camp, hauled it up and nailed it in place, all in one afternoon.

I inherited a double whammy of pioneer blood. My mother Isabel Mary Monro's great-great grandparents settled in Nova Scotia. At the age of seventeen she headed west to teach on the northern coast of British Columbia, met and married Lawrie Lansdowne. The first of ten children came along nine months later. The tenth child came from an orphanage, adopted as a tithe in gratitude for our own good fortune. Though, truth to tell, no outsider could see much good for-tune in our lot. You had to live there, nestled in the great mountains, open to the sea and to the sky.

In the same way you had to live on Rancho Rajneesh to under-stand my gratitude simply to be there. The old pioneer spirit of creat-ing something new and fresh had come alive in jaded twentieth-cen-tury America.

The night before Magdalena cafeteria was finished we gathered for the last time around our icy tables. Our bodies were rigid with cold, the icy wind threatened to blow away our plates, but our spirits were flying. Harida, a short fun-loving Canadian plumber (not to be confused with tall German Haridas, the guard) told us about the earliest pioneers' first trip off the ranch.

"There's only ten of us here then, and this is the first big trip we've organized. We're gonna buy a car at an auction in Madras, ten of us, all jammed into one suburban. We stop in Malkin, everyone bails out to eat dinner and, of course, everyone orders steak and lobster, except me.

"The waitress comes along, she's looking at us, everyone's in red and the mala and she says 'I thought you were all vegetarians.' And I say, 'Listen, let me explain something to you. There's all kinds of vegetarians. There's lacto-vegetarians that drink milk, that's an animal product. And there's lacto-ovo-vegetarians that drink milk and eat eggs. And all sorts of other kinds.

"These guys are *ranch* vegetarians, and right now they're off the ranch!'"

No one could pine for steak and lobster the night that Magdalena opened. The desert air had hit 20 degrees below zero, and everyone stepping onto the heated floor of the mudroom blissed out; our muscles turned to putty, just drinking in the warmth. Such a simple, ordinary thing: ski-cabin warmth.

The huge light space of the cafeteria shimmered as bright red bodies crowded around sparkling white tables, devouring the gourmet vegetarian food. Overnight, Magdalena became the heart of the commune.

On Bhagwan's birthday, December 11, 1981, three months after his arrival, he came to Magdalena to sit with us in silence. This was the climax to which all our effort had been building. Every sannyasin on the ranch came early, scrubbed and shiny.

Bhagwan is wearing a simple white knitted robe and cap. Entering with small, careful steps, he gives the slow greeting that seeks out each individual. He sits, crossing his legs in the old familiar gesture, left over right; then his hands, left over right, resting in his lap. His eyes close. A soughing sound passes through the great hall. Only then does

Lagoons for recycling wastewater and sewage.

it strike me that I too have been holding my breath.

I can't know what goes on in the heart of others. For me there is again the deep contentment, the welling certainty of coming home.

After the push to build Magdalena, the crews zeroed in on Bhagwan's living space and garden. His old trailer was so bad that Bob Davis, a former assistant to the Oregon governor, wrote: "I got a kick out of all the stories about his living in luxurious surroundings—and here he is, sitting in an empty room with a bare linoleum floor and only a chair and a table, and that's it."

He didn't see it at its worst. Chetana came into his room one day to find Bhagwan reading in his chair while rain dripped from the ceiling—Plonck! Plonck! Plonck!—into three pails.

Bhagwan never complained about his room, but once he did mention the absence of trees. Two Dutch sannyasins, professional gardeners, led a crew of novices in a magic transformation of the bleak landscape.

The sound of D-8 backhoes bounced off the rock walls of the canyon as giant machines carved great holes seven feet deep and ten feet across, twice the size of the root balls, out of the rocky slope in

First harvest growing in the harsh terrain of the Big Muddy region.

front of Lao Tzu. From the kitchen window I watched as enormous semi-trucks rolled up the driveway each day for months. Each truck-trailer carried two bundles that looked for all the world like thirty-foot mummified giants.

In every spare moment I ran outside to watch the planting ceremony. Each tree was raised ever so delicately with hooks and chains, lowered into its new home with a century's food supply of specially prepared topsoil, and unwrapped.

The circle of dirt-streaked, sweaty faces lit up each time at the miracle. The lofty trees seemed to shake themselves out and make themselves at home: Towering sequoia three feet across at the base, laden with sprays of fine light green needles; Austrian blockpine with their big cones, looking for all the world like the Christmas trees of my childhood; thirty blue spruce, planted close to his room. "They're Bhagwan's favorite," one of the gardeners told me.

Meanwhile Richard launched an extension to Bhagwan's trailer, a room that Bhagwan designed.

Bhagwan's room was off-limits to everyone except Vivek or her stand-in, the medical staff and the cleaner. Once when Nirupa had a cold Vivek asked me to clean it.

A strange room. The ceiling, walls and floor glowed with mellow parquet. It should have been distracting: parquet isn't often used with such extravagance. But the dark and light patches flowed together in dramatic contrast to the emptiness of the room. A curtained alcove hid the giant bed, a dining corner sported a wood table and two chairs. In the living area stood a table, an upholstered chair, and a stereo system built into a sleek cabinet. The only ornament, a dramatic ebony Buddha, sat solemnly on a many-layered platform.

On three sides glass walls opened onto the new forest. Weeping willows spread their branches over a curving line of pools and streams. The room echoed with the splash of a cascading waterfall that Saguna had helped create in the garden outside. Lines of waving poplars and a grove of silver birch aflame with blue and red ranunculus led my eyes to the distant hills.

The living area reflected the tranquillity of nature; the bathroom exploded into the human dimension. An oversized, pale green jacuzzi filled up half the space. And on its oversized, pale green ledges sprawled in glorious disarray the finest products of the consumer mind: odor-free soaps, conditioners, and shampoos in myriad shapes, colors, and sizes.

Walls and floor of the bathroom were drenched with water. Huge white soaking wet bath towels hung or lay everywhere. Some mischievous boy had spent hours here, enjoying. I mopped and dried, chuckling at the chaos, delighting in the discovery of this uninhibited, fun-loving side of our reclusive master.

As in Poona, Bhagwan stayed in his room day and night. He saw no one during this time except his caregiver, his secretary Sheela, his doctor, dentist and robemakers as needed and two outside visitors— Bob Davis and reporter Kirk Braun. For three and a half years he went out only for his daily drive and rare visits to a completed project.

Those three and a half years of residency in the USA were hard won. Constant legal battles had to be waged with the Immigration and Naturalization Service. When Bhagwan's tourist visa expired, an application was made for his residency as a religious teacher. INS refused this on the grounds that he was at present in silence. On appeal, the Ninth Circuit Court ordered the INS to change their decision.

While the appeal was pending, our lawyers applied under another category, as "a person of some talent and distinction." References flooded in from around the world—in the end a stack nearly six feet high—from theologians, psychologists, lawyers, scientists, police chiefs, film stars et al. No action was taken on this application. And when the Ninth Circuit Court ordered that Bhagwan be recognized as a religious leader, the INS set out to prove that Bhagwan had entered the country illegally, saying he didn't intend to stay when he really did.

But these legal battles were carried on by our lawyers and in no way dimmed the spirit of celebration that infected us all. In July, 1982, the First Annual Festival erupted on the barren hillsides of Rancho Rajneesh.

Communes in Europe, Asia, Australia and Canada had been raising and sending money to support the ranch, their members longing to come. All the sannyasins in the world couldn't live on the ranch, but many of them could come to a party.

For three months the ranch buzzed day and night, preparing a seven-day extravaganza for 5000 people. Boisterous machines tore trenches in the rocky soil for water and sewer lines, and leveled spaces for 1,800 platforms in the sloping valleys. And 1,800 four-person tents sprang up like a field of mad mushrooms.

Like bright helium balloons resting between flights, gaudy canvas eateries billowed up in flat spaces, ringed by gigantic tents housing row after row of gas stoves, each holding its own gigantic shining cauldron or wok. Our new enormous open-sided greenhouse we floored with white linoleum—bumpy but clean—to serve as a meditation hall.

I found my own niche in the festival furor, because by a miracle I had my own car! And with it, yet another taste of Sheela's hatred.

No one on the ranch at that time drove their own car. They were turned over to the commune for general use, including the battered Volkswagon van Saguna had brought.

I'd been slogging through the mud—six inches deep in spots, sucking the boots off my feet; I knew now why the locals called the ranch the Big Muddy—when that same battered blue van stopped to give me a ride. I said jokingly to the driver, "Hey, it sure would be handy to have the old van back to drive in this weather!" We both laughed.

The next day Sheela told Bhagwan I had arrogantly demanded my car back. When Vivek told him my version, he made Sheela personally

Vivek (lower) and Chetana in darshan with Bhagwan.

bring me the keys. The venom in her eyes might have terrified me if I hadn't been so thrilled: to be able to drive again!

The van proved to be just the thing to ferry mattresses, pillows and sleeping bags to the tents for the festival. I sometimes worked till after midnight, caught up in the stunning mix of energy and sound: machines, music, hammering, shouts and laughter, echoing and re-echoing off the rocky canyon walls.

To link the tent sites to the eating and meditation areas, the commune bought and overhauled fifty old school busses. Painted a brilliant yellow, they lit up every heart: now no one would have to slog to the disco or cafeteria through mud in spring and snow on winter nights.

Three . . . four . . . five thousand sannyasins poured in by plane, bus and car from all over the world. As old Poona comrades met and fell into each others' arms, the level of joyous energy soared to new heights and the noise proved too much for the deer; they retreated to the hills. I caught glimpses of them in the morning, lifting their heads, ruminating, gazing down at the strange streams of red flowing into our new meditation hall to sit in satsang with the master.

Each morning for five days Bhagwan came to sit with us. Music of flute, guitar and tablas alternated with humming and with silence. As he entered on the first day in a simple flowing white robe, walking as always with total attention, my breath caught in my throat. So near and yet so far. So human in every way, and yet. . . .

July 6, Master's Day: the pinnacle of the festival. In the afternoon a single-engine plane flies low overhead, scattering millions of fresh rose petals on the crowds in a swirling shower of buoyant, fragile color.

In the evening we wait for Bhagwan in our meditation hall. The sky is dark, ominous; ragged grey clouds rush in from the west. The wind picks up, gusting fiercely through the open hall. Thunder roars through the valley. Jagged streaks of lightning split the sky as Bhagwan's car approaches. As he steps onto the podium, magnificent in a grey velvet robe with full cuffed sleeves, the clouds split open and rain pours down.

Electrified by the storm, we dissolve into a swaying mass of pure energy. The vast hall echoes with our exuberant song: "It is life, love, laughter . . . life love laughter . . . lifelovelaughter . . . awakening!" Thunder booms and rain blows through the hall with each ferocious gust, as if the giant forces of nature are all celebrating with us.

Or could they be warning of storms to come?

Chapter 13

Helpless Hannah

I HAD TO PUSH MY WAY into the packed Wasco County courtroom in The Dalles, an Oregon town eighty miles from the ranch. A lean old man with a lopsided mouth, his face dwarfed by a twenty-gallon hat, was shouting into a microphone. It was hard to make out his words, but the muffled cheers told me he was speaking against the petition of "them Rajneeshees" to form their own city on the ranch.

It was November 4, 1981, my first and only day away from LaoTzu kitchen. An irresistible urge had seized me to attend the public hearing on the incorporation of Rajneeshpuram. I did not believe the petition would be granted, even though many cities in America had been founded by religious groups.

The most joyful years of my pre-sannyas life had been spent in Oregon. In the early 1950's I'd married, lived and worked in Portland; two of my sons were born there, at the full height of the flowering season, every park awash with the scent of roses.

But I knew the state's dark side too. Oregonians made no secret, then or now, of their resistance to newcomers. A popular bumper sticker proclaimed, "Come to Visit, But Don't Stay."

There was no way Oregonians would let us "foreigners" found a new city. The fact that most of us were white and Western cut no ice: We were new, and *very* different.

If a miracle were about to happen, I wanted to be on the spot.

I traveled to The Dalles with two of Sheela's top aides. They didn't talk to me or give me more than a casual, unfocused glance during the trip. This puzzled me; sannyasins usually are very friendly, even with strangers.

In the courtroom the line to the microphone grew as the afternoon wore on. People had come from all over the state to denounce "the Rajneeshees." They spat the word out as if it were poison. The speeches grew ever more inflamed as the afternoon wore on. One speaker after another attacked the "godless heathen" who were "changing our quiet way of life," "getting *our* tax money for *their* city!" Not one individual or group spoke in favor of the petition.

To my amazement the three-man commission of the county court voted two to one in favor of incorporating Rajneeshpuram. Unaccustomed tears came to my eyes. Our city in the desert could happen! The decision gave me a new respect for American justice. I didn't know then how fragile a victory could be.

An organization called 1000 Friends of Oregon, formed to protect the fertile farmlands of the coastal Willamette valley from urban sprawl, campaigned full-out to erase Rajneeshpuram. In the four years after the city's incorporation they launched over a hundred lawsuits, all the way to the United States Supreme Court, which ruled four years later that the city's incorporation in 1981 had been legal and valid.

These lawsuits were to protect land so dry and eroded that, by US Bureau of Land Management standards, it could support only nine head of cattle.

"*Nine cows!*" wrote Ted Shay, professor of political science at Willamette University. "They will go to almost any length to 'protect' the grazing land for *nine cows!*"

But 1000 Friends maintained that the incorporation of a city on *any* agricultural land violated Oregon land-use laws; if the ranch needed any kind of business permit they must request it from Antelope, the nearest incorporated city, twenty miles from the ranch.

Antelope was not yet listed in Oregon tourist brochures as an official "ghost town", but it was well on the way. It had no traffic lights, no hotel, not even a parking lot, and only thirty-nine residents; almost half the houses in the town were listed for sale.

The residents were elderly, Christian and conservative. They didn't want us there. We didn't want to be there. But we had no choice.

Within weeks, rumors of ugly scenes at Antelope city council meetings reached even to isolated Lao Tzu. I went to Magdalena for lunch one day and heard ripples of angry talk amid the waves of gossip. Even from good-natured Rammurti.

"What a pile of shit!" he roared. "They won't give us a permit for a fuckin' hospital!"

A week later a scorching letter came from Shirley, an old friend in Vancouver.

"What the hell is going on down there?" she wrote. "I just saw Sheela on TV. She's so abrasive, shrill, I got furious just watching her. Why doesn't the Bhagwan get someone else to run the commune? You of all people must know there's a delicate PR job that needs to be done, and Sheela is *not* the one to do it, believe me!"

My mind's eye flashed on the possibilities. Many intelligent, beautiful women were on the ranch, able to charm the stingers out of bees with their gentle, courteous ways. I knew at least one had been in public relations before taking sannyas.

What was Sheela telling Bhagwan about Antelope? She had lied about Saguna; maybe, just maybe, the facts weren't getting through to him. Deciding to see for myself, I drove to Antelope for the next city council meeting.

Angry red-clad people crowded the musty council chamber. Two sannyasins who had applied to establish a printing press had been turned down on the grounds of "an inadequate water supply."

"We're not asking to build a laundry!" shouted one, to hoots of laughter from others. "You've nixed our city. That's the only reason we're here!" yelled another.

Council members shouted back at the unruly audience. Mayor Margaret Hall, grim-faced, called for order again and again.

I felt confused, split. We'd been forced into Antelope against our wishes, and in spite of the County Commission's vote granting us a city on the ranch. The council's refusal of services was obvious discrimination.

But my old dream of creating harmony leaped up and shouted. *We should help them understand! Get to know them, help them get over their fear of us. They're old people. They've lived here all their lives. They just need to know us better! And I can help!*

That night I wrote a letter to Bhagwan. Feeling again the flame of enthusiasm, the desire to mould the outer to reduce conflict. My years in social work sprang to life, years of playing the role of Helpful Hannah, determined to solve the problems of the world. . .

"I need to talk to you about the Jacksons," my supervisor said. "You're spending almost half your time with them—helping them clean their house, for God's sake! Remember all we were told about how easy it is to get identified with our clients?"

Clients! That word again, reeking of law and protocol, not an ounce of human warmth in it for a woman on her own with eight kids. The people I saw were stuck fast in a barbed wire fence and I didn't have clippers to cut them loose. Have you ever been stuck in barbed wire? I have. It's one of the most helpless feelings in the world. You can't go ahead and you can't back up. Move at all and you end up torn and bleeding.

Our psychiatric clinic stuck a label on Bobby: constitutional psychopath. No foster home would take a kid with that label. A big blonde boy of thirteen with a high IQ, a birdwatcher, no trouble to his parents or teachers, he had only one problem: he stole cars. New models, powerful.

"Why, Bobby?" I asked.

A dreamy, faraway look veiled his blue eyes.

"I dunno. School's so boring. I love to drive."

I knew that look, that urge to get out from under, to shuck off the restraints of childhood and test my own power; to be free.

On Bobby's third charge I dropped all other work to find a place for him.

Nothing.

He was flung into the sucking maw of reform school.

I felt sick in body and spirit. What kind of society did we have, where a car outranked the life of this beautiful, intelligent child/man?

In a small, isolated community Dorothy, age 14, had born two children to a man with whom she'd lived since she was 11. I had been told to apprehend not only Dorothy and her two babies but her three brothers and sisters, who were well-cared for at home. The school had no problems with them and we had no foster home that would take all three; they would have to be separated.

I phoned the superintendent and told her I did not want to apprehend these three children. But the decision stood: the parents had shown "moral turpitude."

The courtroom was hot and crowded. The judge stormed in.

"I've got a date to go fishing in half an hour," he snarled. "Be warned." He sat down.

Suddenly a fiendish idea blossomed.

I produced birth certificates for Dorothy and her two children, bringing them up one by one to be identified. Then I described our plan for foster care. The judge nodded. But I couldn't find the other certificates. "I'm sorry, Your Honor," I kept repeating, hunting through my briefcase.

The judge's bony fingers drummed on the desktop. Beads of sweat sprouted on his balding head as glorious sun rays, streaming through the windows, overheated the crowded courtroom.

"You'll take the girl and the two babies," he finally snapped. "The rest can go home with their parents."

He rushed out, his black gown flapping behind him. Wire clippers, I thought smugly, come in many shapes and sizes.

But no clippers, it seems, could trim back the ego's great conviction that it can solve *any* problem. In the council chamber in Antelope, listening to the angry shouting, I'd been gripped by the old messianic fervor.

In my letter to Bhagwan I described the fury of the Antelope residents and my feeling that it could be calmed by talking to them, one to one. "There are only thirty-nine residents," I wrote. "I'm a social worker, and if I could visit each house I'm sure it would calm things down. I think they're just afraid of us."

Even as Vivek took my letter down the corridor to Bhagwan's room, an uneasy feeling crept into my stomach. Wasn't this the same old do-gooding that he had poked such fun at? Thinking you can make a difference when in fact you are the problem, the only problem?

According to Bhagwan, do-gooders are miserable and they want to forget about it. The best way is to start thinking about others' miseries. Carrying a thousand and one wounds themselves, still they are trying to help others.

And here I was, after leaving social work because I felt phony, impotent, falling into the same trap: wanting to help, to try a soft sell, a PR number, on the people of Antelope; aching to polish, to smooth over a nasty bump in the road to good relations—a bump that my own intelligence told me was a horrid abscess of prejudice, needing to be opened up. Why should we show respect to a town council so clearly biased against us?

By the time Vivek brought me a word-of-mouth message from Bhagwan three days later, I was in the pits. The delay burned the lesson in deeper every minute. To write such a letter was a display of sheer ego! I remembered his fierce reply to the sannyasin who questioned the beating of the guard in Poona. He would cut me to ribbons.

Bhagwan's response was mild: "Tell Nirgun not to worry. Everything is happening as it should."

But something in the Antelope dilemma continued to pull at me, something too nebulous to wrap my thoughts around. "The mind has to finish what it starts. Be total! Lukewarm won't do!" Bhagwan had pounded that message home, so I sought out Rammurti in Magdalena and he caught me up on the latest.

"Sannyasins are buying houses in Antelope and registering to vote in the city election next month," he told me. "More than half the houses are empty. And you know what's funny?" He grinned a huge grin, his dark brown eyes sparkling. "You know how they don't want us in their town? Hell, the mayor of Antelope is selling houses to us right, left, and center. She's a real estate agent, making a mint!"

"Now they're scared shitless," he told me two weeks later. "Scared the 'red flood' will wash them away." He chuckled. "And you know what? The Antelope council has set April 15 for a vote to *disincorporate the city!* Then we wouldn't be able to get any services on the ranch. Every paper in Portland is full of it. It's the first time any town in America has tried to vote itself out of existence."

On election day I drove to Antelope to witness a town trying to write itself off the map. Norma Paulus, Oregon's Secretary of State, and a senior election officer were on hand to supervise.

A hundred press people jostled each other as they fought for interviews with the voters they outnumbered three to one and tried to frame pictures that didn't include themselves. ABC, CBS, NBC, AP, UPI . . . The familiar logo of the Canadian Broadcasting Company drew me as a red flag does a bull. A great urge came over me to do battle, to uncover the hypocrisy; to tell the world that we'd been forced into Antelope against our will, against the decision of the County Court; that they were witnessing not a "takeover" but a democratic election.

The urge faded as old scenes of impotence flashed before my mind's eye. . . .

1969. The Year of the Token Woman. Business and government raked the country for women to satisfy the first strident cries for equality. I was appointed a director of Canada's billion dollar mortgage corporation, the only woman on a board with nine male directors. But nothing came up within my field of expertise. Politicians were in charge of financial decisions. The Board was a rubber stamp.

Newspaper headlines broadcast a sex scandal: a fellow board member was charged with a homosexual act in a hotel room. When I read this "news" the blood rushed to my face, my hands clenched. What business was it of anybody what others do in the privacy of their own room? I'd fire off a letter . . . Suddenly I realized that I was reading the newspaper, it was my hands clenching, my face flushing. My urge to change the face of society struck me as ludicrous. Who was I, so filled with anger and violence, to suggest how others should behave?

It was 1972. I was in a restaurant having dinner with Bob Andras, the federal minister of housing: a hard worker, a great guy.

"Rosemary," he said, "I've talked to the prime minister. We want you to be our candidate in Vancouver South in the election that's coming up. He thinks you're a natural. And," he added, almost in a whisper, "Pierre is looking for cabinet material. So you see . . . " He broke off and threw out his hands in a gesture that seemed to say "The sky's the limit."

The thought of going into politics repelled me. I started to laugh. "Oh no, Bob. Thank you, but no, no, NO!"

His face turned red. "Rosemary," he hissed at me, "sometimes you have to pay back!"

So there it was, on the table with the remains of the sockeye salmon and Bolla Soave: the hidden agenda. My role in CMHC was that of a mare kept in the stable, fed and pampered, trotted out at election time to show that the government really does give power to women.

My face flushing, tears of humiliation starting, I stood up to leave.

Staring now at the familiar logo of the Canadian Broadcasting Company, listening to the shouts of the cameramen and reporters crowded into the tiny hamlet of Antelope, I recalled those moments of impotence. But they didn't bring back the feeling of humiliation. Instead a new light shone on the message from Bhagwan: "Tell Nirgun not to worry. Everything is happening as it should."

I finally got it. *It's okay to be impotent!* The universe itself is intelligent, conscious. It has given birth to us, it pumps the blood through our body, the air through our lungs. It has given each of us a snippet of consciousness. We need only become more alert, more aware of what each situation calls for, in the moment. We need no plans, no conditioned belief as to what is good, what is bad.

A deep understanding came to me of what until then had been a glib acceptance of his oft-repeated message: our *only* responsibility is to become more aware, more conscious; unconscious actions can only muddy the water.

No action seemed called for that day in Antelope. The facts were all there for reporters who wanted to see them.

Next day I drove back to Antelope to read the newspapers. We had defeated the move to disincorporate; we could approve the services that were needed on the ranch.

Headlines across the United States splashed a single theme: **CULT TAKES OVER SMALL AMERICAN TOWN**. Not one reported that the "takeover" was in fact a supervised election, as democratic and American as apple pie.

The stories didn't stir up even a flicker of anger inside. The strange certainty stayed: everything is happening as it should.

On the way home I saw that our sign pointing the way to the ranch had been shot out and pulled down, replaced by a placard in sprawling letters: **ABANDON HOPE ALL YE WHO ENTER HERE**.

A great sign, I thought, chuckling. An intelligent, creative universe doesn't need our petty hopes, our self-centered dreams. We can all relax.

Euphoria pushed out thought as I drove home, weaving around bumps and cracks in the treacherous county road. Flooded with awe by the sun setting over the endless rolling hills. Drinking in the strong spicy smell of the sage. Living, herenow.

Chapter 14

Dance of Deterrence

OUR NEIGHBOR'S HOSTILITY flamed into the open. In early September 1981 Bhagwan started driving daily to Madras, a town forty miles from the ranch. He parked in an abandoned weighing station on the outskirts to rest and drink a Pepsi, then returned to the ranch.

Soon these drives turned ugly. Vivek came back each day pale and distraught. Normally silent while she made Bhagwan's tea, now she poured out her fears.

"This preacher parks a truck every day where we turn around . . . . waving American flags . . . .ranting through a bullhorn, screaming that Bhagwan is the anti-Christ," she burst out one day, fingers tight around her Wedgewood cup. "He rants on all the time we are there, all the time Bhagwan is resting".

Her stories got scarier. "Truckers are joining the preacher, yelling at Bhagwan, telling him to get out of Oregon while he still can. They've got rifles in their pickups!"

Each day there were more. "They're wearing baseball caps with a picture of a Rolls Royce in the crosshairs of a gun! And t-shirts with Bhagwan's head on them like the trophy of a deer!"

"*Why doesn't Bhagwan drive somewhere else?*" I blurted out. She looked at me a long moment before answering.

"I've asked him already," she finally said, and I saw pain and pride in her eyes. "He says he will not be intimidated."

My heart filled with the same pride. Only a man of conviction and courage could stay calm in the face of insults and threats, could risk his bodily life to keep his spirit intact. He walked the knife-edge of danger to assert the right of individuals to live in their own way, harming no one.

To lighten things up, a cavalcade of sannyasins drove out to the turnaround armed with drums, guitars, tambourines and songs. The truckers were not amused. But a few days later Vivek bubbled into the kitchen. "The sheriff has arrested the worst truckers! He asked Bhagwan, for everyone's safety, to change his route. And Bugsy agreed!" Her face was radiant.

But the hostility didn't go away. Magdalena was abuzz with stories; I didn't have to search for them.

"Did you know a bunch of people have filed a petition asking the state to expel us as an alien cult?"

"Did you know we eat our children?"

"Have you seen the new bumper sticker? ***Better Dead Than Red!***"

"Have you seen *our* new bumper sticker? ***Moses Invests, Jesus Saves, Bhagwan Spends!***"

All too soon the laughter died away. On July 29, 1983, the Rajneesh Hotel in Portland was bombed.

In fact, there were two bombs: the first to bring people running to the scene; the second to blow them to smithereens. It had all the earmarks of sophisticated terrorism, but it backfired. Stephen Paster, the man who set the bombs, blew off parts of his hand and injured his eyes. No one else was hurt. Paster was arrested on the spot and jailed.

Less than two months later, Paster was released on payment of only two thousand dollars bail. I couldn't believe it. How could a US judge let him off so easily for such a vicious crime?

The commune responded fiercely to the bombing. Within days we were summoned to Rajneesh Mandir to watch a video of sannyasins at target practice. The ranch Peace Force officers dressed in mechan-

Main Street, Rajneeshpuram, USA.

ics' uniforms lay on their bellies in long brown grass, firing rifles and pistols at a target.

The real shocker was the target: a life-size human figure made of cardboard, with a heart painted on it. The video was sent to the media to show that we were prepared to defend ourselves if attacked again.

A lively nurse from Vancouver, known to her friends as D.C. because of her six-syllable sannyas name, fought back tears as we talked in Magdalena about the video we'd just seen.

"That *heart* . . . I just feel so bad that my friends have to be doing that to protect the ranch. And yet, maybe we need it. People are afraid of us now; and the way things are, we need that protection."

"Right on, D.C.," I told her. "It's called 'strategic deterrence.' Make the other guy think that if he hits you he's going to get hurt real bad. We're not going to kill anyone, but they don't know that. It's important to fight back psychologically, not just be a doormat. The blacks got nowhere till King got them marching in the streets, picketing, riding the busses."

Amiyo, the feisty American doctor who in Grade 5 had baited school authorities in defence of a black student, exploded into the conversation.

"You guys are from Canada, you don't *know* how violent this country is! Americans *love* guns! My father used to have guns lying around his apartment in New York, he'd wear one in a shoulder holster if we went to the movies in a black area. And out here we're in the Wild West, where there's a gun in every pickup truck. We *need* to look like we can defend ourselves!"

Venu, a long-term pacifist now in the Peace Force, told us she had resisted the target practice.

"I told them my fingers were too small to pull a trigger, but they didn't buy it," she laughed.

I laughed too. "You'll never have to pull a trigger in real life," I told her. "I'm certain-sure this whole show of force is just that, a show, to make outsiders think hard before they decide to attack.'

The show of force mushroomed. Along the county road that wound through the heart of the ranch, guardhouses sprang up, menacing in that isolated, silent setting.

Into this threatening scene in the summer of '83 rode my eldest son Craig; I hadn't seen him since I left for India. I'd told the Welcome Center at the ranch to expect him, and drove down to meet him there. He was alone, and seemed ill at ease.

"Where are Karen and the kids?" I asked.

"They stayed in Madras," he answered awkwardly. "Karen thought it wasn't safe. She didn't want me to come."

I stood there stunned.

"You know, Mom," he went on, "the drive in here *was* pretty scary. Every hut I passed I expected guards to rush out with machine guns."

"They only have walkie-talkies to warn of possibly-hostile visitors," I told him. "And our Peace Force is a legal branch of the Oregon State Police."

I could tell from his face, *Craig didn't believe me*. More clearly than words, his expression told me of the deep chasm between the commune and the outside world.

But he was my son, and we forgot the guards while I took him on a tour of the ranch—astonished myself at what we saw. While I'd been frying dahl and shelling peas in my small kitchen, the ranch had blossomed into a high-tech environmentalist's dream.

Craig's eyes opened wide when we came to the sewage disposal area and looked down on the imposing kidney-shaped basins set in an open valley, where human waste was purified by the latest technology and used for irrigating the hay fields.

The emus at the chicken farm were even stranger. Craig's face broke out in a grin as the huge birds trotted down on powerful legs to greet us, their small fuzzy heads perched on long elastic necks.

I grinned back. "They can't fly, but heaven help the coyote that attacks a chicken," I told him.

We drove past sprawling green fields of alfalfa and winter wheat, acres of bright sunflowers, grapes, fruit trees, never-ending rows of vegetables — an unlikely panorama in this dry and barren county. I held Craig's hand as we walked along the earthen dam at our newly-built Krishnamurti Lake: half a mile of glistening water, tanned bodies on beaches of imported white sand. I pointed out the huge cedar decks and diving platforms that his brother, Saguna, had designed and helped build. Red canoes and sailboats dotted the lake. Craig stared in amazement at the peaceful, beautiful scene, framed by rocky barren hills.

I drove him back to the Welcome Center. As we walked to his car my mind stormed with thoughts: *How to convince him that we would never fire a gun at any living creature?* I knew deep down it wouldn't be possible; the fact that Karen and the children had not come showed how deep was their fear. But shouldn't I try? And then the thought flashed: *Maybe it isn't good to convince him. The whole strategy of deterrence depends on everyone outside believing that we mean business.*

I relaxed into the moment, into the great warm hug Craig gave me before he left.

"I'm glad I came, Mom," he said simply.

Toward the end of the summer, the lake was the scene of a freak accident. Amiyo was swimming when it happened.

"I had no idea what was going on," she told a table of eager listeners the next day in Magdalena. "All of a sudden somebody was yelling through a bullhorn to *get out of the water!* We all swam to shore and huddled there, rumors flying. The Portland Hotel bombing was still on everyone's mind and somebody said there was a bomb somewhere. It was pretty tense for a while. Then I saw Harida drive up with scuba gear and word spread that someone had drowned."

Harida broke in. "Jesus Christ! What a scene!" He snorted, continuing the tale in his unique laugh-your-way-to-God style. "The water was really muddy, I couldn't see my hand in front of my face. Swimming in the muck, looking for a body, it was freaky. I was sure by that time he'd be dead.

"All of a sudden I felt this hand and I grabbed it, and then *it grabbed me*. Oh shit, it grabbed my leg and I nearly died. It was someone else searching. He had to let go first because he didn't have oxygen, and he bobbed out onto the surface saying, *I've found him and he's alive!* And then I bobbed up and said *No he isn't, that was me*. We looked for another twenty minutes before someone found him and we hauled him out. They did the whole bit with artificial respiration but it was clear he was dead."

Harida paused, then shook his head.

"It's gonna take a couple of days to get a coroner to come and declare him dead and make sure we haven't poisoned him or cut his head off—you know, all those horrible things everyone thinks we do to anybody—and get in touch with the family in Japan and get permission to cremate him.

"So at noon yesterday it's stinking hot out, 105 degrees—they had him in the medical center and I told the nurse, 'Jesus, this guy's going to be really ripe by evening.'

"They've got him in the back room with this pissy little air conditioner blowing, with all the doors open. She wants me to cook up some refrigeration to cool this man down and I said, 'Put him on ice!' We thought of putting him in the Magdalena food freezer. . . ."

"Can you imagine the scene when the cooks walked in on him in the morning?" someone interrupted to roars of laughter.

The joking shocked me. Other people were doubled up with laughter, listening to Harida's story. But their hilarity didn't feel right to me.

"What's the matter, Nirgun?" Amiyo gasped between chortles. "Don't you think it's funny?"

I shook my head. "I've always felt the dead should be treated with respect."

"That's the way we're brought up," she said, sobering. "But respect doesn't mean you can't see the funny side. Remember the story of the dying Zen master who hid firecrackers in his robe so they'd explode when he was cremated?"

I remembered that one, also Bhagwan's famous cat joke about death and the uneasy laughter I'd choked back when he told it.

At the cremation of the swimmer we welcomed death Bhagwan-style as the climax of life, with song and dancing.

Rays from the setting sun lit up the red rock walls of the isolated canyon where we celebrated the burning of our dead. Shadowed crevices transformed the surface into a gigantic abstract painting; it was a majestic site, full of silence. The sun rays bounced off the shining copper cone of the crematorium that jutted into the sky like a volcano on Mars, a space ship ready for launching. A magical place to say good-bye to a loved one.

On the surrounding slopes a crowd of red-robed sannyasins stood in silence, swaying gently to a quiet guitar and flute melody. The firewood had already been laid, covering the entire body. The touch of a match, and flames roared up. Musicians broke into song and sannyasins joined in, swaying, dancing, faces lit up by the fire, the music, the mood of celebration; singing the simple words.

> *Walk into the holy fire,*
> *Step into the holy flame.*
> *Walk into the holy fire,*
> *Step into the holy flame...*

Blazing light covered the hillsides, turning the red-clad bodies into living, moving flames. As the music faded I existed for a timeless moment in a different space, watching myself turn to move with the throng crowding toward the buses. Again came that wash of knowing that I am not my body; that life is a continuing adventure, an infinite opening through the door of death into a great unknown: a mecca for a pioneer spirit.

Chapter 15

Dynamic Devices

M AGDALENA CAFETERIA BUZZED like a swarm of red bees.
"Wow, Nirgun, what do you say? Think we can do it?" Rammurti asked as I slipped into the chair beside him.

"Do what?" I asked. I was often out of the gossip loop.

"Finish building the city in two months? Or so." He grinned.

"What?"

"You really haven't heard? Wasco County won't give us any more permits or extend the ones we have when they expire. Everything that's started—the hotel, the townhouses, the reception area, the shopping mall and restaurants, the bar and lounge—we have to finish them all, now."

"The Crunch," as it came to be known, was on. It was late '83, winter was close upon us. Workers from every department threw themselves into construction, leaving only skeleton crews to manage cooking and cleaning. Lao Tzu was no exception. Those in the commune who had seen Bhagwan's house staff as special, living so close to the master, now saw us leap from sewing sequins to screeding concrete. I mastered my fear of heights and got into the rhythm of firing staples into shingles on slanting roofs. Ker-*choing!* No boss, no orders, just keep moving, keep firing. Ker-*choing!* Early morning, November, dark, frost warning: DO NOT SLIP! Ker-*choing!* Ker-*choing!*

Waiting for shingles one morning before dawn, I looked out over the chaotic flood-lit site where townhouses were leaping to life, seeing familiar faces intent on unfamiliar work. Samiyo, a teacher from Vancouver, was overseeing the cement pour in the second townhouse. He wiped sweat off his forehead with his arm though it was cold out, then guided an enormous cement truck between the holes and swung the chute around, only a few inches to spare on each side. Women were running vibrators, puddling the quick-drying concrete.

Beyond him a ranch photographer, lean and dark, coaxed a yellow crane to lift the floors and then the walls trucked here from our shed/factory. The floor lowered onto its new concrete foundation, the walls jerked up and were caught, guided, secured in place by nailguns in the hands of a dozen eager amateurs. Floor joists would go on next, on top of the walls, then the upstairs walls; then the roof—tricky stuff. But the face of the photographer was relaxed, smiling. He moved the levers of his huge machine with confidence. The staccato of nailguns, the buzzing of skillsaws echoed in the frosty air.

On the other side of the townhouse where I lay spread-eagled, the roof was already on. Through windowless gaps I saw Haridas and helpers putting in pipes and wiring in the upstairs rooms. Downstairs a bevy of women, protected by ballooning orange coveralls and gloves, rat-a-tatted prickly yellow insulation to the two-by-fours. Close behind another crew fired nails into creamy gyproc.

Sound came from all directions, fast and furious as machine gun fire; no place, no time for talk. The shingles arrived. On my solitary roof I picked up the staple gun and added to the chaos. Ker-choing! Ker-*choing!* Ker-*choing!*

Magdalena at lunchtime was a softer chaos, awash with laughter. The strenuous cold morning work had charged the batteries of sedentary workers like me. I looked for Amiyo. Her big mouth stretched in a great grin as she hugged me.

"Wow! Nirgun, I can't believe it's happening!" She choked on a hot chili. "Coming here on the bus, we saw *four new townhouses!* All roofed and windowed! The whole bus cheered."

"The electrical inspector from Madras is here full-time, we keep him so busy," Sarlo, her long term companion, put in. Reserved, thoughtful Sarlo—now his blue eyes were shining with fun in his tanned face. He'd been gripping a carpet stretcher since six a.m, kicking out wrinkles as the tough cheap carpet went down.

"Aren't you tired?" I asked.

"Not a bit," he said. "It's exhilarating. I'm a lazy person ordinarily, I've always worked as little as possible." I believed him, he still had the beard and the hippie vibe.

"Working for money is selling your soul just to keep your body together. Now I'm working for the fun of it." He laughed. "With Bhagwan you always know it's a game. Here the aim is to test your limits: do something you've never done before and do it fast and *well*."

"Boy, that's the truth," chimed in Samiyo, who had been doing the cement pours. "It totally blows my mind, it takes every ounce of togetherness I've got. When Saguna asked me, I thought I couldn't do it," He grinned at me. "But it had to be done, he trusted me to do it, so I did."

"But it's the women who really get off!" Amiyo interrupted. She'd been perching on the edge of her chair, dying to butt in. "There's such a feeling of freedom in doing things men have always done. Driving caterpillars, tractors, backhoes, and those enormous D8s!"

Rammurti sat down next to me at the table. "So, you guys heard the latest?" His voice sounded ominous. Everyone stopped eating.

"OK, listen to this. Yesterday Dave Frohnmayer, the Attorney General of Oregon, declared that our incorporation is illegal because we have no separation between church and state."

"Bullshit!" Amiyo almost shouted. "What about the Mormons? What about Salt Lake City? Jesus Christ, what a load of crap!"

"Just let me finish," Rammurti said calmly. "He says he's going to file a lawsuit against us."

"You see?" cried Amiyo, her hazel eyes sparking, her pale face flushing with rage. "What have I been telling you? The American government wants us out of here! You Canadians are so innocent, you don't understand. This country is run by right wing fundamentalist nuts!"

"Come on, Amiyo," Sarlo laughed. "We've all heard your conspiracy theories before."

"It's not just the government," Amiyo told him, her face now intent and serious. "Look, I grew up in this country. I have family in Madras. Some of those people who were yelling at Bhagwan in Madras were *my relatives.* They think Bhagwan is the Anti-Christ and they're doing the work of Jesus by trying to run us out of here. My little nephew had to be *rebaptized* after he sat on my lap and chewed on my mala!"

We all laughed at that, but uneasily.

"I don't know, Amiyo," I said. "It sounds pretty farfetched to me."

"Then why is the Oregon government going to court against us, Nirgun? Why are they going to so much trouble to get us off 64,000 acres of worn-out land when the only harm we're doing is bringing millions of dollars into their fucking state?"

Silence followed her explosion. I thought, *It's a reasonable question.*

Sarlo broke the silence by pointing to his wristwatch: 2 p.m, time for "Driveby," when workers lined up along the road to watch Bhagwan drive out. No bell sounded, no foreman's voice called out. The cafeteria crowd dissolved out the door like a swarm of minnows seeking a sunlit shallows after a heavy feed.

As The Crunch moved toward its climax, all sites were floodlit at night, work mushroomed to fifteen, sixteen hours a day. We staggered through layers of fatigue and resistance to find the fabled "second wind." And then a third. The Crunch pushed us all beyond our boundaries, shattered our belief in the tiny limits of our energy.

Commune members had barely moved into their new homes—centrally heated, complete with toothpaste, shampoo and hand lotion—when another crisis erupted in our lives.

Snowdrops were just beginning to poke their noses out in the sheltered space next to the Lao Tzu trailer; it was now the early spring of '84. White peacocks strutted on the back porch, preening in front of the huge windows in our living room. Turanti was feeding them bits of our tea snack when the door burst open and Devaraj strode in through the mudroom. One look at his face and everyone stopped eating. Usually ebullient, now he was deadly serious. He started to talk while he poured himself a cup of tea.

"You remember what Bhagwan told me last month about AIDS?

That it would become epidemic and wipe out two-thirds of the world's population?"

Snug in the Oregon desert, we hadn't bothered much about new diseases or grim prophecies.

Devaraj squeezed into a space on the sofa. "Well, now he's given us sexual guidelines, to keep it from destroying the commune. Sheela's going to announce them tonight at a public meeting. Our first choice is celibacy."

No one could relate to this but me. To the others it was obviously an impossible choice, they were still kicking over the traces that had harnessed them for so many years. But in my mind the thought flashed: *Why not take Bhagwan seriously? He's always said the reason for going totally into sex is to go beyond it.*

"If celibacy isn't possible without repression," Devaraj went on quietly, inexorably, "these are the measures to be followed: no sexual intercourse without condoms; surgical gloves for any intimate sexual contact; no mouth-to-mouth kissing; shower before and after sex; blood tests for everyone, every three months."

We looked at him to see if this was one of his jokes. But he was deadly serious. Chetana froze with her cup in midair. Turanti turned white. Haridas and Asheesh simply stared at Devaraj, unbelieving.

Even I was appalled by what they faced. Rubber gloves would destroy the spontaneity, the freedom, the intimacy. The idea was revolting. Years of shucking off sexual repressions, and now this?

I took the uneaten apple crumble back to the kitchen, wondering how I would feel if the sexual dance still held me in thrall. Washing the dishes I started to laugh, seeing how smugness crept in with age. Remembering the hilarious scene when the dance ended for me. . . .

After my marriage crumbled, I often flew to Ottawa for CMHC Board meetings and conferences. Frequently the only woman in a male world, I had a wide choice of companions and wasn't often alone in my luxury hotel rooms. The sensuous carpets proved a delight not only to wade in but to roll in. At age forty-seven my sexual energy exploded like a bursting nova.

In Ottawa Foster became a frequent companion. He prided himself on his sexual stamina and versatility, and it was no idle boast. We tried out every posture in the Kama Sutra, at least the ones that were physically within my abilities.

But I got bored. Not just with Foster, with rutting; with the rut of rutting.

One evening I came into my hotel room to find a silver vase overflowing with spring flowers. Red tulips, purple lilacs and white narcissi filled the room with fragrance. And on the dresser lay a melange of plastic objects, in all shapes and sizes, from a simple white rubber with a corrugated surface to an elaborate, colorful rooster's head.

"French ticklers," Foster said, a note of pride in his voice.

I cracked up then, laughed and laughed and laughed, rolling on the thick chocolate carpet—alone and for the last time. The absurdity of that collection of condoms turned me off. Somehow their absurdity spilled over onto the sex act itself, made it seem unreal, plastic, unnatural. I'd been bored before; now my whole body/mind shouted, **Enough!**

Washing the tea dishes in Bhagwan's kitchen, I chuckled at the memory. But laughter was a scarce commodity on the ranch that night. When I picked up the Lao Tzu staff at our meditation hall after Sheela's general meeting, everywhere subdued groups were huddling together for support. No one spoke a word on the way home.

Spirits grew lighter as sannyasin humor took over. Devaraj and the nursing staff staged a raw skit on safe sex, using a sheet with holes, a huge carrot, and dialogue that evoked gales of laughter. A female sannyasin worked all day dressed as a condom, rubber from head to toe. Other measures had a touch of the aesthetic. The staff of the ranch hotel prepared exquisitely wrapped and beribboned boxes for each room, boxes filled not with chocolates but with condoms, gloves, wipes.

Lewd reminders were kept in-house, like the song that ended

Always use rubbers whenever you screw
And wash yourself thoroughly after you do.

The commune stocked our trailers with KY jelly and regular French safes, and stocked the pharmacy with the fanciest imported condoms from Switzerland and Japan, gossamer thin, silky, in blue and pink.

After the initial shock Turanti greeted the new regime with great good humor. She'd been with the same man for more than a year, but she still loved to tease.

"I like to walk up to the pharmacy window and ask for condoms," she told me. She was my pipeline into the sex life of the commune. "All the men laugh. I ask them which type they prefer, and they argue about it. Of course they offer to try them on for me. But I wonder why they don't come in flavors?" She wasn't joking.

"Rubber condoms don't taste good. At first I couldn't get into oral sex. But I missed it, it's such a great part of the foreplay. My taste buds just had to get reconditioned."

Turanti found another plus. "It's difficult for a man to stop and put on a condom," she told me. "But if a woman puts it on her partner and follows it with oral stimulation, it's a loving way to encourage him to take precautions."

I couldn't help thinking that public health officials dealing with AIDS outside the commune should learn to talk in this no-nonsense, encouraging way. And coming from Turanti!

"It's hard to believe you were raised a strict Catholic," I told her. Turanti grinned. "It is funny, isn't it?" she said. Her sparkling brown eyes turned soft. "Maybe some of the repressing got cancelled out by all the loving I got from my mom."

Two months later an even stranger furor erupted on the ranch. Suddenly everyone had to report to Pythagorus, the medical center, for an eye examination. Many cases of conjunctivitis had broken out, we were told; Sheela was afraid that Bhagwan might become infected.

Having no symptoms, I decided not to go. But when I heard that Vivek and Devaraj were already in a trailer hastily converted into a ward, I blasted off to the medical center to find out what was happening.

Pythagorus was a madhouse, packed with a milling crowd of sannyasins talking and laughing while they waited. A harried doctor peered into my eyes and told me that, yes, I did have signs of conjunctivitis, I'd have to go to the ward with the others from Lao Tzu. I noticed that he looked into my eyes all right, but he didn't look me in the eye when he spoke to me.

"But I don't have any crustiness, my eyelids don't stick," I argued. "They feel perfectly normal. And how could so many people get infected all at once?"

He insisted. "There is a slight redness, and no precaution is too great where Bhagwan's health is concerned."

I went out to sit in the van and look at the facts. Something was not right. Only Sheela could contrive such a massive scam, but what for? No answer came, but no sense of danger either. The orders were preposterous but not life-threatening. Ego bashing was routine in the commune—anything and everything to destroy an individual's feeling of being superior. This was the first time LaoTzu had been included in an ego bashing, but so what? I thought jauntily. Why should we get off scot free? We weren't special.

I found most of the staff from Lao Tzu in the trailer/ward, playing cards. Nirupa had stayed in Lao Tzu to look after Bhagwan. The rest of us relaxed in the sun, enjoying, gossiping. We all knew the eye infection was a scam: Welcome to Club Con! More "patients" came in, reporting that dozens of trailers had been turned into wards; more than half the ranch residents showed signs of conjunctivitis!

We were "released" on the third day.

When we went got back, LaoTzu was full of Sheela's moms. They were scrubbing walls and floors, dusting ceilings, muttering and scowling. They didn't look at us, didn't speak to us though we'd been together in the commune for years. A big blonde was scouring the shower in our bathroom, scouring and muttering, "This is disgusting! Awful!"

It felt as if our rooms had been ransacked by thieves. Immaculate clothes had been washed, the silks totally ruined. Every gift from Bhagwan was gone: a covered tea mug he had used, towels, pictures, my huge green sheet that he had slept in.

Turanti hissed with anger. "We've been pulled out of our house, stuck in a ward for no reason, now they've destroyed our clothes and stolen our gifts!"

My gifts from Bhagwan had disappeared too, but it didn't seem so important to me. Bhagwan had spoken many times about the need not to be attached to anything, not to possessions or to him.

The intruders left. Later the phone rang: it was Dolma, saying she and some other moms would be up at seven o'clock to talk to us. I relaxed; Dolma was a friend.

But it was a phalanx of Hitler's army that arrived at our door that night. They marched in, stern of face, ten of them, carrying a tape recorder. It took them a long time to set it in the right position in the exact centre of the table, then test it. Somehow the sight of a tape recorder unnerved me, made the meeting seem like a trial.

Venu, my fellow Canadian and pacifist friend who had resisted target practice, seemed to be in charge of the group, and I relaxed when I saw her. Perhaps half my age, slim and blonde, with innocent blue eyes, she was not at all intimidating. But tonight she spoke and acted as prosecuting attorney.

After a few brutal remarks about the general slovenly condition of the house, she turned her full attention to me—the chief criminal. Her voice rose, full of venom.

"The kitchen is a disgrace, a menace to our Master's health. The sink and cupboards are a disaster, filthy and greasy and stained; grease is running in streams behind the stove . . . and the freezer!" Venu paused, groping for words to express her horror. "An atrocity, that *this* should be in Bhagwan's kitchen, this jumble of bags, open bags, everything spilling out! The whole kitchen is a pigsty," she cried, her face wrinkling in disgust, her voice rising, her blue eyes flashing fire. "You, Nirgun, he has trusted you to cook for him. That you could endanger his health, his very life. . . ."

Frozen into silence, I sat and listened to the charges, sensing every eye on me, condemning, cold; not daring to look around; feeling the rush of pain, the anguish of being alone in a hostile world.

I almost never cry, but suddenly tears were gushing down my cheeks—tears of helplessness, of humiliation. Everything in the kitchen wasn't perfect, I *was* careless: towels hung carelessly, the dishcloth hanging under the sink instead of out on the line, the sink stained from yesterday's tea leaves. Compared to Turanti and Nirupa and Chetana, I was a slob. They were all so *meticulous.* I was really sobbing now, all my hidden feelings of inferiority surging up, swamping me. *They're all so beautiful and young, What is an old careless hag like me doing here?*

Venu's fierce attack picked the scab off ancient humiliations never addressed, and the pain poured out. I couldn't stop crying.

Suddenly I became aware that my housemates were crying too, in sympathy and silent rage. In their supporting tears I felt my connectedness. I wasn't separate; I wasn't alone.

Vivek suddenly stood and announced she was going to ask Bhagwan to cancel the meeting. She slipped out the door as she spoke.

Her swift action brought me back to the practical world. I took Dolma by the arm and half-led, half dragged her into the kitchen. She didn't want to come, kept repeating, "We should get back to the others. We're not supposed to leave the group." But I held onto her. "See for yourself!" I cried as I pulled her from the sink (one tiny tea stain) to the stove (one spot of grease on the catchpan) to the freezer. The packages in the freezer were not precisely stacked, and six loose peas glared up accusingly from the gleaming white surface.

But I didn't feel guilty anymore. I'd come to my senses, just looking into reality. How could anything in a freezer threaten Bhagwan's health anyway? I'd been put here and I was doing the best job I could. *So what if I'm not meticulous? Cooking is a messy business. So is life*, I thought, letting Dolma go, washing my bloated face in the sink, drying it on a dish towel.

Vivek announced that Bhagwan had cancelled the meeting. The gestapo left. Later in the kitchen she told me what Bhagwan had said: "Couldn't even one of you have replied, 'Oh, is that the way it seems to you? I'll certainly look into it, and if you're right I'll be sure to thank you.'"

For the first time these simple words penetrated. He'd told us so many times, in so many ways: *Reaction is from the ego, from your conditioning. Don't react, respond. Check out reality. Use your intelligence.* Venu's fierce energy, the sudden sharp humiliation had triggered a reaction; my prickly ego was alive and well. Only later had I responded with intelligence, looked into the facts.

The real-life drama drove home the point as no words ever could.

In bed that night I became aware of a strange gratitude toward Venu. By playing her role as fascist chieftain full out she had shocked me into seeing how I flinched from criticism, how I clung to my superior image, how I became lost in emotional storms. And now I knew I could come out of any storm, simply by checking out reality, seeing what is.

Obviously Venu enjoyed her role; that's why she had gravitated to Sheela's gang. But I felt that she had played the part knowing it as such, believing she was carrying out Bhagwan's shuck-off-the-ego teaching. Nobody had been hurt, only my pride had been wounded.

Turanti came into the kitchen next morning and we talked over a cup of tea.

"In all these years I've never seen you cry before, Nirgun," she said. "Sheela and her moms are off the wall. Why don't we complain to

Bhagwan? I'm sure Vivek would take a letter to him."

"In Poona Deeksha used to pound on you and you knew it was a Zen stick," I told her. "Sheela's moms just use a sledgehammer. If we stop buying into their game and don't get upset or suck up to Sheela, she won't have any power. Vivek has told Bhagwan everything." I gave her the bare bones of his message.

Turanti didn't argue. But events were to prove that her intuition was also true.

Chapter 16

"Chaos and Confusion are My Methods"

*I*N THE SPRING of 1984 a new group of residents appeared on the ranch. Rich, cultured, sophisticated, able to lavish gifts on Bhagwan, the Hollywood set drove Sheela crazy with jealousy. Hasya, John, Kaveesha and David arrived en masse and en Rolls Royces and lived together in a mountain A-frame. When Hasya and Devaraj became lovers she often came to Lao Tzu.

As coproducer of *The Godfather*, Hasya had won world recognition. But she put on no airs. Her brown hair flowed straight to her shoulders, framing a pale heart-shaped face and serene, attentive eyes. She bought Bhagwan new and expensive fabrics for his robes. Her own "castoffs" she gave to the girls in the house, and they delighted in the lush velvet and silks. Girls will be girls in castles or in communes, and the extravaganza of the Third Annual World Festival was close upon us.

This was the first festival after the Portland Hotel bombing. Our show of force was devastatingly total. Cars preceded and followed

Bhagwan on his daily drive, guns strapped dramatically to the doors. A helicopter roared overhead. The menacing line of guardhouses doubled; a guard dog sniffed the bags of every visitor for drugs.

When they first arrived on the ranch, visitors from abroad were often amazed and disturbed by the weapons; they hadn't lived through the open hostility, the bombing.

To me the sight of our armed readiness brought a fierce joy. I was glad, glad that we were not about to turn tail and flee in the face of intimidation. The bigger show of arms, the better, was the quixotic thought of this sixth generation Quaker. The only defense of the truly nonviolent is psychological resistance. The arms were a symbol of our determination to defend our way of life, the only symbol a violent foe could understand.

A twelve-foot electric fence sprang up around the double trailer where we lived with Bhagwan. A thirty-foot tower soared above us, manned by armed guards twenty-four hours a day. At Sheela's insistence, Vivek detailed the house staff to walk nightly around to check for intruders.

This 'defense' to me had the flavor of a surreal sham. Lao Tzu sat on an open hillside of red rock and stunted juniper; a small plane with a single bomb could blast us all into our next life. But I knew also that 'the play's the thing,' our only safety, and so I crept stealthily in the pitch dark through the prickly Mungho pines, stepped silently over the slippery rocks.

Harida and Venu were now part of Sheela's scene at Jesus' Grove, and they served as guards in the tower that soared over our trailer, brandishing semiautomatic guns. I caught them at lunch and put my question to them. Since the evening when she had verbally annihilated me, I felt connected to Venu in some mysterious way. Raised in a choice section of West Vancouver, she had been a flower child and a dedicated pacifist. Her role as armed guard seemed out of character.

"Venu, would you really fire one of those guns at someone?" I asked her.

"I haven't faced up to it yet," she admitted. "We're trained to use them if there's a real threat to Bhagwan, but I've never been able to imagine firing at a real person."

I looked at her quizzically. "It's not just me, either, Nirgun," Venu said, almost defensively. "Three weeks ago someone got into the grounds above Bhagwan's house and walked right up to his window. And the guys in the tower didn't shoot. Sheela called a big meeting and tore them apart—talk about ego-bashing—because they didn't fire. The whole reason for the tower was to protect Bhagwan, but they didn't even think of shooting."

Harida broke in. "It's just as well. Some of the guards couldn't hit the broad side of a bull's ass with a bass fiddle!"

The show of arms intensified when Bhagwan came to sit with us during the festival in our meditation hall. Guards stood in a metal crows nest in the ceiling rafters, rifles at the ready. On either side of the podium, flanking Bhagwan, a guard posed motionless on one knee, his Uzi cradled in firing position. I cheered them silently.

When Bhagwan went out on his daily drive the sight was even more ludicrous. The car hood was piled with roses, placed there by sannyasins as he drove by at 2 mph. Solemn, serious, unsmiling, a guard with an Uzi stalked ahead, grimly surveying the waiting line of sannyasins. A helicopter circled overhead. The bizarre combination of Rolls Royces and rifles, roaring helicopters and roses brought the theatre of the absurd to new heights.

Bhagwan had been creating a spectacle with his Rolls Royces for years. Early in 1982 we had printed in the Rajneesh Times a photograph of 29 of them lined up in a curving row. The news spread. In India Bhagwan had been dubbed "the sex guru." In America he was nicknamed "the guru with the Rolls."

Bhagwan didn't stop at twenty-nine. By the end of our time on the ranch he had at his disposal ninety-three Rolls Royces, all the same model, the Silver Spur. They were housed in bunkers in the hillside below Lao Tzu, out of sight. Bhagwan gave the artists of the ranch a free hand to paint them any way they chose.

The Rolls made headlines across America in what author Tom Robbins called "The greatest spoof ever staged on American consumerism." I could have hugged him for that felicitous phrase.

Each day a different Rolls was featured in "driveby," when sannyasins greeted Bhagwan in a line by the side of the road. As he was still in silence and gave neither discourse nor darshan, this was the only time, apart from festivals, that we saw him.

At the Third Annual Festival in July, as if in response to the threatening look of guns and guards, sannyasins began making "music" during driveby: pots and pans and drums and flutes and shake shakes and noisy singing. Anything that could express the joy and exuberance we felt. The car slowed to a crawl; the mechanic had to install a special fan to keep the motor from overheating.

Bhagwan would stop in front of an especially lively group and wave his arms, encouraging them to ever greater heights of speed and musical insanity. The chaos of sound, bereft of any resemblance to a musical performance, lambasted all within earshot. This was an energy darshan, Western style, in the great outdoors.

Each day during the festival Bhagwan crept by in a white/red/purple/striped/decorated Rolls Royce, smiling his special brand of magic, driving and conducting. The line of laughing, crying, celebrating red bodies stretched along the road as far as the eye could see.

But the real theater of the absurd started in late August of '84. I caught my first glimpse when Nirupa and I went to the corral, an outside dance floor less crowded than our standing-room-only discos. Unfamiliar men lounged against the railings, smoking. One of them yelled at Nirupa, "Hey, honey, wanna fuck?"

We didn't stay.

"Who are they, Nirupa?" I asked as we walked back to Lao Tzu.
"I've heard that we're busing in homeless people from all over America," she said, "but I don't know why. It's no fun coming here anymore," she added sadly.

That was all; Nirupa wasn't one to gossip.

Sheela had sent sannyasins to all major cities in the United States to seek out homeless men and women—in soup kitchens, parks, and derelict hovels—to offer them an expense-paid trip the ranch. The program was dubbed Share-A-Home. Hundreds, then thousands swarmed in, in huge buses with a sannyasin host, from New York, Miami, Los Angeles, San Francisco, San Diego, Chicago, Boston, and Washington. But why? Magdalena buzzed with guesswork. Was it a generous urge to share what we had with those in need, as Sheela said?

"Charity work has never been Bhagwan's thing!" Sarlo laughed when I asked him over lunch.

"Could be a spoof on do-gooders," I suggested. "Bhagwan has said that charity is a way of keeping the poor quiet and the elite in power."

"No way, Nirgun," insisted Rammurti. "Sheela's bringing them in

A floating pavillion at Krisnamurti Lake.

to vote in the next Wasco County election!"

A roar of agreement greeted this, a chorus of "That's it!" "Dead on!" "Everyone knows what Sheela says about it is bullshit."

Heads nodded enthusiastically up and down the table. Things like that weren't often said openly on the ranch.

"But just what has she got in mind?" cried Amiyo. "I've looked at the figures and there isn't a hope in hell that the Share-a-Home votes could influence the election. Sheela's just crazy. Give me a break!"

"I'm taking a break for my beer." Sarlo stood up. "You want yours now?"

Suddenly to understand didn't seem important to me. In fact, not to understand with the mind was the name of the game. It was an intuition rather than a thought. "Chaos and confusion are my methods," Bhagwan had told us in Poona. How else to shake us out of our static state?

Sheela confiscated all pistols, knives, chains, and knuckledusters. The newcomers were outfitted with ranch clothes. They worked along with the rest of us, ate the same food, drank the same single can of beer at supper, danced in the disco, goofed it up at driveby, slept in our crowded trailers and A-frames and insulated tents, and got more than their share of dental and medical treatment simply because they needed it.

Shock waves rolled through the commune as the numbers of Share-A-Homers swelled till they seemed to outnumber the residents. Some of the newcomers were indignant at the very idea of working, of not smoking inside buildings, not spitting or throwing garbage in the streets. Many left within days. But many others stayed to enjoy the vast open space of the ranch, the plentiful food, the friendly openness of sannyasins—though that friendliness was strained to the max by the huge lineups for medical care and by the gross appearance and actions of many of the newcomers.

I asked Saguna if having a Share-a-Homer live in his trailer had caused any problems.

"Po, mom," he said, the commune word for yes and no. "He does make a lot of noise at night, snoring and hitting the wall. But," he added with a sly grin, "Elli and I are in love, so we make good use of the time."

Some sannyasins felt uneasy about Share a Home.

"Going dancing later, D.C.?" I asked one night as we headed down the path from Magdalena.

"I don't think so," she answered. "It's not comfortable anymore. There's a vibe—it just doesn't feel like our community anymore."

I thought about that as we walked on. D.C. was right, things weren't the same. Our tight egghead commune had been lumbered with an almost equal number of the "great unwashed." For me it was a vital shake-up, but D.C. was a bit of a worrywart. We walked on in silence.

"You know, Nirgun," she added suddenly, "that used to be one of the best things about this place—knowing you were safe in all situations. It's not just the way some of the men snigger at women. I'm a little afraid of them, period."

Alarmed, I asked, "Has anyone touched you, roughed you up?" D.C. was an attractive woman.

"No," she said slowly. "It's just a feeling."

I breathed a sigh of relief. We didn't need the threat of violence inside the commune, we were getting enough from outside. For two years US navy jets had made sporadic flights over the city, low, noisy, and somehow menacing. In the past months they had become more aggressive—one skimmed the runway of our airport without contacting the tower and zoomed away.

One morning during discourse two navy jets dived on our meditation hall—once, twice, three times. The roar was deafening, threatening, brutal. Bhagwan sat quietly, smiling, unperturbed; continued his talk after the jets screamed away. After discourse I heard a graying sannyasin tell a small group, "That's what they did in Vietnam. They called it 'buzzing the gooks'."

The coming of the Share-A-Homers had intensified the smouldering rage against the commune. Public meetings bristled with "Bhagwan Search and Destroy" t-shirts, shouts of "Kick him out!" "Send him back!" "We don't want them taking over our state or any other state!" Rumors of massive armaments on the ranch abounded. Rumor control telephones were set up and operators reported two to three thousand calls the first day.

To dispel the fears of the public and quell the most common rumors, on October 17 the Oregon governor published a fact sheet in *The Oregonian*:
1. The Rajneeshees have one helicopter which is not capable of holding a machine gun.
2. State officials saw no buildup of arms in the city.
3. 15% of the Share A Home "street people" had left, about 3500 remained. There had been no crime wave in the area.
4. There was no evidence to indicate that Rajneeshee children were abused.
5. There were no Rajneeshees receiving welfare or food stamps.

The operations commander of the Oregon State Police told *The Oregonian* that the Rajneeshpuram Peace Force was an authorized state police force.

But other government agencies did not take this cool, factual approach. More than thirty federal and state agencies met behind closed doors "to discuss emergency plans for dealing with the Rajneeshees." Included were two agencies, the FBI and The Bureau of Alcohol, Tobacco and Firearms, later officially probed and censored in the fiery deaths at Waco. The Rajneeshpuram Peace Force was not included.

In the fall a heavy cold and cough forced me to leave the sanctuary of Lao Tzu for three weeks. During that time I worked cleaning up the garden beds around the Multiversity, my silent work punctuated by shouts, screams, laughter and music from the therapy groups. A rangy blond, a loner like myself, joined me in the work.

"What brought you here, Jim?" I asked him one tea break as we relaxed on the grass. He took a long time to answer.

"I'd been working the strip in Las Vegas for thirty years," he said thoughtfully. "The place was getting too hot for me. And suddenly this bus comes along offering a free holiday on this big ranch in Oregon, and I just hopped aboard."

He was one of the Share-a-Homers! "What do you mean, working the strip?"

"Dealing in the gambling houses," he told me. "Dangerous, but it pays well."

"You're a professional gambler?" I asked, still unbelieving.

"Since I was thirteen," he said. "I worked for a butcher who shaved the sides off cubes of meat to show me how to make flat top dice, just enough to beef up the chance of rolling those lucky numbers. I made my pocket money in high school with flat tops."

Next day I heard about angry gamblers and sweating pursuit down dark alleys.

"I used to carry a pistol always," Jim said, running his hand ruefully under his arm. "Sheela's gang took it away from me when I got here."

After my return to LaoTzu I sometimes dropped in on Jim in his trailer after supper. Any doubt about the truth of his gambling tales disappeared one day when I found him asleep on the sofa. I touched him lightly on the shoulder and he sprang to his feet, knocking me away, his hand flying into his armpit.

One evening in the late fall I found him sitting on the veranda of the trailer. Wearing a mala.

"It just happened," he said simply. "I was standing in the crowd as he went by, and this time he slowed down and really looked at me. I mean, it felt like I was the only person on the whole damn road." He looked a bit dazed. "My name is Adarsh now."

I hugged him in delight.

He leaned back in his chair and stared upward for a long time. I stared too. The night was spectacular—so many stars, so bright in the vast dark solitude.

"You know, Nirgun," he said softly, "if there is a heaven, it must be something like this."

When Adarsh asked me one night if I knew any girls who might like to go out with him, I asked Saguna for suggestions and got a put-down laugh.

"Nobody here is into prearranged dates, mom," he told me. "Shit happens, and so does romance."

More than six months after he came to the ranch, Adarsh suddenly decided to leave. He'd been working in construction and wanted to set up a small business in Seattle with a sannyasin friend. I took him out to dinner at the mall.

"What's with this sudden plan to leave the ranch?" I asked him bluntly. "I thought you were happy here."

He exploded like a lighted gas jet.

"Anything is better than the stuff coming out of Sheela and her moms these days! It makes me want to puke. Ranting and raving in the ranch meetings, tearing people apart." He shrugged in disgust. "Making everyone wash their hands in alcohol to prevent AIDS, for God's sake!" He paused, then added in a lower voice, "And the guns, Nirgun. I might just as well be back on the strip, there's the same feeling of danger in the air."

No one could argue with that. I tried to explain the need to look armed and dangerous but he shrugged impatiently.

"I don't care what you say, Nirgun, things round here are getting heavy. Sheela's just crazy."

His tone was so determined I knew he'd made up his mind. We ate for a while in silence. He seemed uncomfortable.

"Nirgun," he said, "I'm going to Seattle this week with my friend. He has enough money to get started but I don't."

"How much do you need?"

"Three hundred."

I nodded in relief. "That's OK, Adarsh, I can give you that."

Adarsh just looked at me, his thanks plain on his face.

He left the ranch the next day, I never saw him again. But he left me with a question. I had defended Sheela's outrageous behavior to him, to Turanti, to myself: Sheela was the Zen stick in Bhagwan's hand, to batter our encrusted egos. Now I wondered if the Zen stick had taken on a life of its own, just as the bamboo stick had in my Poona garden. Had grown into a tree with ugly branches and poisonous fruit. If all was well in our garden, why would Adarsh want to leave?

Chapter 17

Something is Rotten

*T*HE HUGE DESERT SUN, low in the sky on an autumn day in '84, transformed the square glass bottles of dahl into a dazzling display of tiny jewels. Through the window beyond them I saw Sheela's Mercedes wheel into the driveway and stop in front of the door to Vivek's room. Sheela helped Vivek up the stairs and into the house. Moments later Devaraj rushed through the kitchen and down the corridor.

Alarm bells rang in my head. Vivek was never sick. Frozen into inaction, I waited till Devaraj came back through the kitchen. My anxious look brought only an expressive shrug.

"We don't know what's wrong, Nirgun," he said. "But it looks like she'll be off work for a few days . . . ." and he was out the door.

Three days later, pale but determined, Vivek was back on the job.

"Whatever happened, love?" I asked her. "It was so sudden!"

"I went to see Sheela about some Bhagwan business," she told me. "She was amazingly friendly, chatting, making me a cup of tea. And suddenly my heart started to pound, I felt weak all over. Sheela wanted me to lie down, but all I could think was, 'I've got to get back to Lao Tzu.'"

"Does Devaraj know what caused it?" I asked anxiously. She still looked far from well.

Vivek looked at me, then answered slowly, emphasizing each word. "I know what caused it, Nirgun," she said. "Something in the tea. Sheela put something in my tea."

I couldn't speak. We both distrusted Sheela, but this? Finally I burst out, "Vivek, not even Sheela is daft enough to pull a trick like that!" Vivek shrugged her shoulders. She laughed, a forced little laugh. "No one believes it. I hardly do myself. But I won't drink tea with her again!"

Six days later, after three and a half years of public silence, Bhagwan began to speak again.

Before entering into silence in Poona he had spoken to the full commune every morning. Now meetings were held in the evening, in Lao Tzu, in the small living room of his old trailer; it could hold only fifty people. The house staff and some therapists could attend every night; the rest of the commune came by invitation on a rotating basis.

New soft drapes billowed around the windows, shining new wood covered the old floor. The space was small, intimate; each night we pressed together, filling every inch of the room.

On that first night Bhagwan speaks slowly. It seems an effort.

"These days of silence have helped me to find my real, authentic people who are not in need of words to be with me," he tells us. "Communication is through words, and communion is through silence.

For the first time I am speaking to my own people: not to Hindus, not to Mohammedans, not to Christians, not to Jews."

The old fire comes back as he goes on to lambaste all religions, taking special aim at Christianity.

"The concept of God in all the old religions is out of fear. The people who believe in God are really people who cannot trust themselves. They need a father figure, a Big Daddy!" His eyes are flashing now.

"*Jesus was not a Christian!* His only crime was that he was himself an individual, trying to live authentically his own way of life, not bothering much about tradition. He had to die on the cross just because he insisted on being an individual.

"More blood has been shed by Christians than by anybody else; more wars have been fought by Christians than by anybody else. People have been massacred, butchered, burned alive by Christians!"

My spine tingles as he speaks. Rejoicing to hear the lion roar again. Prickling with a sense of danger. These are bold words in Ronald Reagan's America.

I rejoiced too the day Vivek told me that Bhagwan had lost enough weight, his back was greatly improved, and Indian Mukti would come in to cook Indian food: chapatis, parathas, rasmalai. Delight flooded me. I'd starved our beloved master back to health, he could eat all the foods he loved! He was speaking again, I could hear him every night— or could I? Vivek answered the sudden alarm in my eyes.

"Of course you're still Keeper of the Kitchen, you'll still live in Lao Tzu."

Those who lived outside the master's house didn't fare so well. After Bhagwan began to speak again, Sheela's ego bashing flared to new heights. Rammurti sought me out one sparkling winter day in Magdalena.

"I know you can't help me, Nirgun, but I need to talk to you," he said. His face looked oddly old, strained. We went outside and sat on a log by the creek. The sunlight showed up the dark circles under his eyes.

"Last week I was told to leave. No debate, no question, no appeal. Just pack my bags and get out; I was negative, and that was that. I was shattered and shocked, crying and weeping." He paused, his eyes misting with tears. I couldn't think of anything to say.

"I went through hell the next four days. It was like an encounter group only in real life. I went to Jesus House and saw Sheela, told her, 'I do have a dark side, my humor always comes out cynical, negative. I know it's important to look at my negativity, but I want to do it here, with Bhagwan.'

"Sheela slithered out, sent me back to the main office to see Vidya. I had to go back four times: She sent me to see one mom, who sent me to another, who sent me back to the first mom. And of course they were never there, that's the way they work, you have to chase them.

They tighten the noose around your testicles each time.

"The fourth day was really traumatic. I'd been pegged as negative. All of a sudden people stopped talking to me, thinking if they were seen with me, they might be next.

"Then just walking down the corridor, I passed Vidya and she called out airily"—he imitated Vidya's airy-fairy voice—"'Oh, it's fine to stay, Ram. As long as you just don't be negative, everything's fine.' After four days of torture . . . that's the way they do it."

I put my arms around him and hugged him, hard. I'd gone through an hour of ego bashing; four days seemed an eternity.

"What do you make of it all, Ram?" I asked. I still hadn't got it entirely straight—such a ruthless humiliation. But he'd looked into what was happening.

"Around Bhagwan there's these profound types of events that happen, people are playing roles. It's very hard to comprehend in the moment, and that's the beauty of it, Nirgun. If you can comprehend the device, it won't have any effect on you. Then you can outsmart it. And with a wiseguy like me, always a step ahead of the game, it has to be something pretty devastating or I'll slide around it. So I got my ass kicked around because I was the harder type.

"My conclusion is that if you're sincerely here to wake up, all that has to happen will happen for you. And the more receptive you are, the more situations will arise to help you clear the deck."

I took a deep breath. Ram was saying so clearly what I'd always felt. But somehow the ego bashing seemed to be getting more severe, almost sadistic.

"Why are you telling me this now?" I asked him. His forehead wrinkled.

"I guess because things are getting even crazier around here," he replied. "If they change their minds and I have to leave the ranch, I want Bhagwan to know what happened." He looked at me, entreating.

"Ram, I don't think Sheela has the power to kick you off the ranch," I told him. "She wasn't able to prevent Saguna from coming. Just get word to me, I'll send a message in with Vivek." His face lit up.

When I got back to LaoTzu, I suddenly saw it with new eyes: a prison. The high link fence, the gates that delivered a powerful shock; the guardhouse towering over us, manned round the clock by two still figures holding guns—until this moment I had seen them as a deterrent to hostile outsiders. Now they seemed to be directed against us, the sannyasins who lived in Bhagwan's house!

Sheela couldn't hassle us directly as she did Rammurti. We were Bhagwan's house staff, she couldn't threaten to kick us off the ranch. That's why she hates us! The certainty struck me. We're the only people on the ranch outside her power. She could only harass us—the charged fence was her prod, and the armed, silent guards perched in their aerie. And the bugging. . . .

Turanti had noticed it first and hit me with it one summer afternoon while I was sitting on the clover lawn, watching the blue-gold peacocks preen and rattle.

"Nirgun, do you know that our phones are being tapped?"

I must have looked skeptical.

"It's true," she said. "I've suspected it for a long time. Yesterday I phoned Mom in Vancouver and told her about slipping off with Didi for a walk in the hills. And today Nirmal ripped me apart for leaving work with 'Didi'! How could she know my private name for him?"

"But bugging is a big job, Turanti—wouldn't we have suspected something?"

She had pulled me over to the electric fence that ran behind the peacock house. A freshly covered trench ran the full length of it.

"What do you think that is? I've heard the wires go down to a special trailer in Jesus Grove where Jagruti monitors everything."

Soon word flowed through the gossip loop that other houses were bugged too, including those of the Hollywood set. No one took it seriously. I heard that each night before he went to bed John wandered around the house shouting "Up yours, Jagruti!"

Finally even Turanti had laughed. "Bugging doesn't matter when you have nothing to hide," she said.

And I thought, that's right on. To have nothing to hide is a great freedom.

Now suddenly the bugging, the fence, the guards felt part of a plot. Was I getting paranoid? For a week the guards in the tower hadn't smiled or spoken to us. They didn't drop by for tea anymore, or even ask to use our bathroom.

I knew one of the guards from old Poona days. Next time he passed by the house I fell in step with him.

"What's with the deep freeze?" I asked him lightly.

He looked straight ahead and kept walking. But from the corner of his mouth I heard, "Sheela's orders."

"Did she say why?"

"She says it isn't good to get friendly with people you might have to shoot."

The shock of his words stopped me in mid-stride. Was this just another Zen hit, or something more sinister? "Sheela's just crazy!" Adarsh had said. What if he were right?

My mind churning, really suspicious now, I went to the next Sheela meeting. She called them sporadically, but I hadn't gone to one for more than a year. I didn't like her and had good reason not to trust her. If we all refused to attend her meetings, I had reasoned, her power would fade.

At this meeting, the viciousness of her attacks shocked me to the core. She baited plump and friendly Sushila, known to us all as a dynamo at raising money for the commune.

"Look at that flab!" she sneered. "No wonder you don't have a lover." We sat in silence, transparent fear in every eye: Will I be next?

But when she switched her attack to the outside world, her audience warmed. In vivid, vulgar words she described Oregon officials as irretrievably evil, out to destroy a commune that was the highest and best the world had ever known. I was stunned, not so much by the nastiness as by the applause that followed every accusation. Shocked most of all by my own response: even knowing Sheela as I did, I had to sit on my own hands to keep them from clapping.

It's the Fourth Annual Festival, July 6, 1985. The enormous meditation hall overflows: 15,000 disciples have gathered to sit in silent communion with their master. We are unusually sober. In every country the rumble of the coming storm has been heard. The anger of church and state—inflamed by Bhagwan's ridicule and Sheela's outrageous tactics, fanned by media headlines—threatens to explode. The suspense has thrown many into the present, fiercely determined to live each moment as it comes.

Noises of the outside world do not penetrate here. The silence is deafening, throbbing with life. Morning sun rays turn the rocky hillsides into a golden cathedral.

Bhagwan appears on the podium. A hushed gasp, more felt than heard, greets him. Showman extraordinaire, his robe is a theatrical "Star Wars" costume of black and gold with shoulders accented to look like embryonic wings. The full sleeves, solid with gilt sequins, complete the illusion as he raises his arm. A glittering gilt band circles his black hat like a crown of fire; the skirt of the robe is embroidered with purple and silver.

He greets us as always, making eye contact slowly down each long row. Minutes pass. Then he sits in the chair, crosses one leg over the other, folds the left hand into the right. His eyes close.

Silence.

Music erupts. Startling music. Not the soaring, evocative strains of flute and sitar as in the past, this music is chaotic, abrasive: cymbals and heavy drumming, a blaring trumpet. I am stirred by its sheer raw energy, and disturbed by it. The music seems to reflect the harsh reality of the world we are living in.

Again, silence.

Taru, an enormously fat Indian woman with the high, sweet voice of a child/angel, stands and sings an old Buddhist chant.

Silence.

Devaraj reads, a short selection of Bhagwan's words. He sits at the back beside the musicians and the microphones. His exquisite delivery, his resonant British voice command attention. The huge gathering is still, as if Bhagwan himself were speaking.

Silence. Again, the wild abrasive music.

Bhagwan rises, namastes, leaves. I sit on, listening to the silence filling with sound—rustles, whispers, movement as the throng of sannyasins comes back to this life.

I hear the sound of running feet, feel a surge in the crowd. An ambulance careens into sight, pulls up at the far end of the hall. A murmur starts: Devaraj. Devaraj is ill. They're putting him in the ambulance.

When Vivek came into the kitchen I wheeled around. Her face was pale, her eyes wide. I ran over, put my arm around her.

"Is it . . . is he . . . ?"

"He's in the medical center, Nirgun," she said gently. Vivek knew my soft spot for high-spirited Devaraj. "He's coughing up blood. He's still in danger, we have to send him to the hospital in Bend."

"What happened, Vivek?" I shook her gently, urgently. "How could he suddenly collapse like that? He's such a healthy horse. What does he say ?"

Vivek looked at me, tears filming her wide eyes. "That's the worst part, Nirgun," she whispered. "The doctor just told me. Devaraj claims he was injected with poison, by Shanti Bhadra."

Poison. The impossible word sank slowly into my mind, then into my body, paralyzing it. Poison!

And Shanti B! Bright and bubbly, mother of two happy, healthy teenagers, a sannyasin since Poona days; one of Sheela's group now.

"Not Shanti B," I whispered..

"I know. It can't be true," Vivek said. "But the doctor saw a puncture mark and fresh blood when he was brought in."

I looked at her in unspoken question.

"Bhagwan says we need to get more evidence."

When she came through the kitchen again she told me, "He says we shouldn't gossip about it till we have more facts." And that was the last she had to say about the poisoning.

The Hollywood set believed Devaraj. He was flown the same day to the hospital in Bend, Oregon; Hasya, Kaveesha and David drove down and one of them stayed with him every moment, day and night.

Flat on his back in the hospital, Devaraj tried to collect evidence. He asked Maneesha to pick up his clothes from the ranch medical center; they would surely show signs of the injection. After a day's delay they were handed over by one of Sheela's moms.

Sure enough, the underwear showed where the fabric had been pierced, a small stain the color of blood surrounding it.

But in the pocket of his robe lay a bag check ticket, attached to an open safety pin. Of course! That explained it! The safety pin had opened during the celebration and pricked Devaraj!

We all wanted to believe this, so badly.

Maneesha drove to Bend and told Devaraj the news of the pin with great delight. She was met by angry bellows.

"You're crazy!" he shouted. "Do you think I don't know the difference between an injection and a safety pin? Look for yourself!"

He pulled back his nightgown and displayed on his buttock a small bruised area with a tiny puncture mark. He tried on the robe, showed how no pin in his pocket could have reached that spot.

But Maneesha didn't buy it, couldn't believe it. Devaraj stopped trying to convince anyone.

None of the staff in LaoTzu believed his story, not after the pin came to light. It would have turned our world upside down. We had to deny it. Even my mind, predisposed to think the worst of Sheela, bought the pin-prick theory. Vivek stayed mum.

Devaraj came home, but not as the robust, hilarious housemate he had been; he was pale, quiet. The sun had gone behind a cloud, a pall hung over all of us.

Since the July festival Bhagwan had been giving morning discourses to the entire commune in our meditation hall. On the day Devaraj came home from the hospital, he began giving evening interviews to the international press in Jesus Grove, Sheela's headquarters. These meetings were small, by invitation only; I went every night.

On the evening of Friday, September 13, Bhagwan referred to a letter Sheela had written to him a few days earlier, saying that she no longer felt so excited when she returned to the commune from her trips abroad. I looked around; Sheela wasn't present.

"Perhaps she is not conscious," Bhagwan told us, "She does not know why she does not feel excited here anymore. It is because I am speaking and she is no longer the central focus. She is no longer a celebrity. She is still a celebrity in Europe, but here all that has disappeared from her life.

"Deep down all those who have power will not like me to be here alive, because while I am here nobody can have any power trip."

It was a huge hit for Sheela, in front of sannyasins and a half dozen reporters.

Next day I was in the mall pizzeria when a burly sannyasin threw the door open.

"Sheela and her moms have flown off the ranch! Packed up and gone, for good!" he shouted.

A wave of relief flooded through me. More than relief, exhilaration: To live without the bombast, the negativity, the ugliness—through the open door I heard a growing murmur as the news spread. Sannyasins poured out of the shops, collected in small groups, shouting, laughing.

Reverberating through the mall, the rusty tones of an accordion began to play:

> *Ding dong, the witch is dead!*
> *Which old witch? The wicked witch!*
> *Ding dong, the wicked witch is dead!*

over and over, louder and louder. The street swarmed with singing, dancing, cheering red bodies. I knew most of the dancers.

My exhilaration faded as a new insight flared.

A vivid, mind-boggling memory: They'd been at Sheela's last meeting—cheering, shouting applause. And I'd had to sit on my own two hands. To keep them from clapping.*

---

* A rumor came from Down Under that, on Sheela's visit to Australia, drugged drinks had been given to board members of a company she wanted to take over. Later, we heard that the water of a school in Karrie Valley had been poisoned—but by then the Oregon commune itself was reeling from one shock to another.

Chapter 18

Power Failure

OUR MEDITATION HALL overflows with red-clad bodies; sannyasins clap and sing to the music of violin and strong percussion. It's the morning after Sheela's sudden departure. Looking around at the crowded hall I think: We're all here, celebrating like kids when the school term finishes.

Bhagwan comes in smiling, waving his arms to conduct the musicians. The hall turns silent as he sits down and folds his hands, left over right.

"I can see you are all immensely happy." This enigmatic opening is greeted with tentative laughter and clapping. "I came to know just a little late that you were dancing in the streets, otherwise I would have joined you." Loud laughter, clapping. "I myself am feeling for the first time at home." Louder laughter, cheers.

"Few more things. . . ."

These "few more things" will shatter the Oregon commune.

"Just the other day I came to know," he tells us in his usual quiet tone, "that Sheela and the whole gang that has escaped from here were trying to kill three people who are very close to me: Devaraj, my physician; Devageet, my dentist; and Vivek, who has taken care of me for all these fifteen years."

As his words penetrate, the vast crowd becomes absolutely still. One paralyzing phrase stands out: Devaraj . . . poisoned! I have known it in my heart from the first moment.

Bhagwan continues the devastating recital.

"Things were repressed out of fear. People who knew could not say, because saying meant they would be thrown out of the commune, and they did not want to leave me. One sannyasin has told that there was a meeting a few months before. Vivek, Devaraj, Devageet, all three should be killed by slow poisoning."

Bhagwan describes Vivek's sudden collapse. "It took three hours for medicine to bring her heartbeat back to normal. This has never happened before. She had taken only one cup of tea at Jesus Grove, and immediately this happened."

"Sheela wouldn't be so daft," I had said to Vivek when she told me. Why hadn't I believed her?

"In the meeting here Devaraj was injected with poison. He immediately understood what had been done. He started saying he had been poisoned. Nobody could believe it."

Not one of us who lived with Devaraj had believed him. Why not? Why couldn't I see the truth? *Because the truth would have put an end to my role as pioneer in a far-out spiritual utopia! Founder of a new way of life, a model for the world—superior!*

The insight strikes with lightning force. Like everyone else I have been lost in dreams, not seeing the ugly reality that would be clearly visible to unblinkered eyes.

Every fiber of my being is alert now as I listen to Bhagwan. "You will be surprised and shocked that even my room, my sitting room, my bedroom, were all bugged." This is hilarious. Bhagwan bugged? Whatever for? A joke?

The urge to laugh vanishes in a flood of shock with his next words.

"I have heard that some government office in The Dalles was burned, and it was the work of this group. It is just a rumor that they tried to poison the whole of The Dalles' city by poisoning their water system. They did not succeed, but they made the attempt."

Burning government buildings? Why? Because politicians were unfriendly to our city? Poisoning a town's water supply? For what? To prevent a whole city from voting? Is Sheela insane, a monster capable of doing anything to get her own way?

My mind leaps from Sheela to Bhagwan. *He put her in charge. Did he know she was capable of such crimes? With his wisdom, his knowledge of the human condition, couldn't he have foreseen her actions? Couldn't he have stopped her?*

Everyone asked these questions; some put them in writing. Bhagwan answered them day after day in discourse.

"I had chosen Sheela to give you a little taste of what fascism means," he told us. For years he had poured out warnings that obedience is the greatest sin. That our need to obey, to forsake our own intelligence and follow blindly—follow parents, politicians, priests—is the root of fascism. Till this moment these had been mere words. Now he pounded in the truth arising out of our own experience, right here, right now.

He told us how and why devices are needed. "Truth cannot be said to you. You won't understand it. You are fast asleep, snoring." Christ's message to his disciples flashed into my mind: Wake Up!

"I create devices outside your bedroom," Bhagwan went on. "For example, I may scream that your house is on fire. When you come out and see the sunrise and the birds singing, you will be grateful to me, although the house is not on fire."

But why Sheela? What could we learn from her?

"What happens when people come into power? Whatever they have been carrying in their unconscious, now they have the opportunity to materialize it," Bhagwan explained. "So from this experience you have to learn one thing: Somewhere deep down you may be carrying Sheela and the whole gang. The only way to know whether it is really there is to give you power.

"It is not the power that corrupts. Corruption is in you. Power simply gives you the opportunity to show your real face. So power is not your enemy; it is a mirror.

"Power gives you the insight to become aware, to help you destroy the Adolph Hitler within you."

I knew it already, deep down. In Poona Bhagwan had given me an authority role so that I could see, hidden behind a mask of humility, my unconscious desire to dominate. Was the ranch a device for us all to play with our power trips?

"Sheela was only one side of the story; you are the other side. Without you she could not have been, and done ugly, criminal things.

"You are blind, you are in darkness, you live in unconsciousness. If I had not told you what Sheela was doing, you would have completely lived under her with no problem. . . ."

Why didn't you speak out?

The accusation hit me like a thunderclap from the sky.

Who, me? I tried to defend against the attack from within: I'm old, and a woman, and I hate fighting. Sweat trickled down the back of my neck.

But you had the best opportunity to bell the cat! You lived in Lao Tzu, Sheela couldn't throw you off the ranch. You knew hard facts of her deceit, her lying to Bhagwan, her nastiness to workers. You escaped, stayed away from her meetings. 'Don't rock the boat!' Coward!

Over and above the inner brawl I heard Bhagwan's words.

"I also knew that I can start speaking any moment, when I see that things have come to a peak and they have to be stopped . . . The experience will make you more responsible, less dependent on authorities."

It was true! We had lived for years in chaos, lived at full throttle in a volatile world, sharing our money and labor without holding back. No one had been killed, no one permanently injured.

A great resolve arose in me: to take the experience to heart, to act according to my own intelligence, not outside authority. No matter what my fears. No matter what the cost.

That resolve would carry me into deep waters.

Fiery debate raged through the ranch as sannyasins wrestled with the existential questions now thrown at them.

"I take full responsibility," said Harida, his strong words catching the attention of all at our table. "It doesn't matter if you were out in the Dalles poisoning people or working in the electrical department like me, people were compromising themselves. Ninety-eight percent of the people were just as guilty as anyone else. People say to me, 'Oh, I never would have done that.' As far as I'm concerned that's just bullshit, absolute crap. If they'd been given the opportunity they'd have taken it and run, just like everyone else. It's just like Hitler's Germany. . ."

"That's it!" Deva Allen broke in. "Now I realize what Hitler was all about. I remember when I was a kid my father trying to explain to me how people could follow this madman. It never made any sense to me. But when you've surrendered your own judgment, your own power. . . ."

His voice trailed off.

"We all did that," D.C. said softly. "We all did it. I always had such a superior attitude about the German people who lived under Hitler and supported him. And now I see that I'm the same as the average German who lived in the average house and let all that happen. I'm such a sheep."

"You're not the only one," said Harida. "We all did things that deep in our hearts we knew we shouldn't be doing. We accepted it for whatever reason. You were afraid if you didn't do it you would be asked to leave. Or you would lose your position, you wouldn't be able to stand up in front with the gun so everyone could see how great you were. Or you thought, 'This is coming from Bhagwan, I should go along with it.' So pick your reason, you compromised."

"It just didn't occur to me," sputtered D.C., getting excited, "it just never occurred to me to trust myself. Whenever I was around Sheela's moms I always felt bad, but I thought it was because there was something wrong with me: I'm not smart enough, I'm not responsible enough. Through the whole thing I thought, well, Bhagwan put them there, it must be right."

I jumped in. "But he always says, Don't listen to me, don't obey me, don't obey anyone. Just listen to your inner voice and follow it. He's never contradicted that. Dozens of times he's said that obedience is a dirty word."

"Yeah, he's said it all right," agreed Harida. "But you can't sit in a lecture and get it just like that. You have to live it before you wake up to what you're doing. From the first year I thought, Why? Why is this fucking zany stupid woman in charge here? And now I think maybe we needed her."

"Maybe we did." I pondered that one. "I think Bhagwan would do almost anything to help us wake up."

Saguna took the revelations hard. He caught up to me one day as I was walking back to Lao Tzu after lunch. We hadn't seen each other for days and I started when I saw him. His face was pale and unsmiling, his shoulders drooped.

He must have seen my reaction because he smiled, a bleak smile.

"Mom, I have to tell you," he said. "Elli and I are leaving. We're flying to Vancouver the day after tomorrow."

"Is it because of Sheela?" I asked. His attempt at a smile vanished.

"The commune is coming unstuck, just when we'd got it all together." There was no mistaking the bitterness in his voice. He'd poured his heart and soul and streaming energy into building our beautiful city in the desert, loving the challenge, the camaraderie. The thought of his leaving, angry and disillusioned—close to tears, I wheeled to face him.

"What about Bhagwan?" My voice came out a whisper. "Are you mad at him? Isn't he the real reason we're here? To look into what's going on inside, no matter what he throws at us?"

It took Saguna a minute to answer.

"Since we've been on the ranch Bhagwan hasn't been available like he was in Poona," he answered slowly. "A minute at driveby, seeing him at festivals, and I've had one invitation to listen to his discourse in LaoTzu." He smiled, joylessly. "It's different for you, Mom, you live in his house, you get to hear him a lot." He paused. No words came to me.

"I just don't feel the old closeness somehow, you know? It feels right to go, not cling to the past. Elli feels the same."

I clung to him for a long minute. He had to tear himself away.

After Saguna left, my urge to understand grew more intense. What possible motive could Sheela have for these bizarre attempts at arson and murder? How could she hope to get away with it anyway? Hadn't she seen that it would bring the whole commune tumbling down? My mind went bananas till I remembered the revelation that came to me three years ago in Antelope: my only responsibility is to become more aware, more conscious of any hidden motives in my own actions.

Night after night I went to hear Bhagwan as he continued to meet with the world media in the Jesus Grove conference room.

To a question about Sheela's tendencies Bhagwan replied: "Everybody is capable of doing something like that if so much opportunity is given. A person has so many faces—did you think when America had chosen Nixon there would be a Watergate?"

James Gordon, a writer and psychiatrist who had been coming to the commune for years, called our master-and-disciple relationship a game, the M.A.D. game. "You played because you wanted to, at your own risk, for exactly as long as you wanted."

At the nightly press conference in Jesus Grove, Gordon asked Bhagwan why, knowing Sheela's insensitivity and ruthlessness, did he entrust his commune to her?

Inside the conference room no foot shuffled, no chair squeaked.

"It is not a question of thinking pros and cons," Bhagwan told him. "It is my insight. Looking at the world, I could not give the commune into the hands of innocent people. She served her purpose perfectly well."

These strange words blazed in my mind like sheet lightning. Of course! Who but Sheela, with her tigress ferocity, her tough don't-take-no-for-an-answer inflexible will, could have brought about this city in the desert? She had created a perfect stage for us to taste the fascist fruits that grow out of the urge to power, a taste never conveyed by words. We had experienced here and now the growing ambition and violence of leaders, the sheep-like stance of followers.

"You play a very risky game, Bhagwan," Gordon responded thoughtfully.

"Certainly," Bhagwan agreed. "I'm a very risky person, and it *is* a game. I know the right timings. I'm just a referee."

Life soon got riskier. The American authorities had been looking for an informer inside the commune. Now they had the biggest and the best: the Bhagwan himself. I sat in discourse, dumfounded, as he invited them in to investigate Sheela's crimes. They responded with a vengeance.

They came in droves, set up a trailer, manned it day and night. Oregon State police, Wasco County officials, FBI officers, the Attorney General's deputy, National guardsmen, INS officers. They flew in, drove in, camped overnight; stayed for weeks. I counted fifty searchers on the ranch in one day. They ransacked offices and trailers, questioned, subpoenaed residents. Dug up suspect plots, brought in the Navy Seal divers to search the mucky bottoms of Krishnamurti and Patanjali lakes.

While they rifled and dug and ransacked I did some investigating of my own. Sheela had bugged Bhagwan's room, but why? How? I knew who could tell me and found him in his trailer, strumming, singing. He was a gentle, introspective musician, passionately devoted to his master and an expert in all things electronic.

"One day I was told to make a very small box with an emergency call button and a hidden microphone underneath," he told me. "In the world of spies you don't want to know too much. But I guessed, because it had to look really nice—"

"Why did you do it then?" I interrupted. "If you suspected it was for Bhagwan's room?"

"I thought he might be in some danger from the people closest to him," he answered slowly. "You know, when people get close they can build a bigger ego, and then they have to face bigger fears inside."

With a start I remembered Shiva. I'd heard a rumor that he was writing a book called *The God That Failed*; he'd left the ranch when he lost his special status as a Lao Tzu guard. And Astha! The commune grapevine reported that she was now testifying against Bhagwan to the FBI.

They had both lived in LaoTzu.

"Sheela thought the Hollywood gang was a threat," my spy friend went on. "I knew that Hasya had coproduced *The Godfather*"—his eyes turned up, remembering. "I thought they just might be connected with the Mafia."

"But how did you do it?" I insisted. "He's always locked in his room at night, Vivek brings up the key. Who could have walked in and planted a bug in broad daylight, with all the staff and guards about?"

He grinned sheepishly. "What did you think the conjunctivitis scam was all about, Nirgun?"

The massive search and interrogation kept on, and on. Rumors of Bhagwan's imminent arrest flooded the commune. Starting to fear for his safety, I risked a question to Vivek.

"Have they charged Bhagwan with any crime?"

"No," she said simply. "The FBI made two appointments to interview him and then canceled them. Bhagwan insisted that the interviews be videotaped."

A risky game—I could barely grasp the outlines of it. The ranch crawled with press and police. Bhagwan had invited them here. Why?

A reporter asked him, "Are you a publicity hound? You enjoy the fact that your words are transmitted to all these people?"

"I love it," Bhagwan answered. "Because I am not going anywhere. I am a contemporary man; why should I not use the whole media that is possible, to spread the word?

"There are millions of people around the world who may not ever come in contact with me. But through the media some of them may get a glimpse. A few of them may even come. My message is not limited to any group of people. It is for all human beings as such. So I want to reach all the nooks and corners of the world."

My mind's eye sees again the green grass of a park in my distant past, sees a wild dancing figure, a swirling locket, a tiny picture. My first glimpse.

At lunch in Magdalena, Rammurti corralled me in a quiet corner. "The news out there is bad, Nirgun." His voice was quiet but urgent; his sardonic grin was gone.

"There's a high-level conference happening in Madras right now: National Guard, Oregon State Police, FBI and other government agencies. They're talking about invading the commune."

"What on earth for, Ram? Sheela and her gang have left. . . ." His silent fear reached out, choked off my words.

"They're out to get Bhagwan and the commune, not Sheela. The National Guard have put at least a dozen armored vehicles around the ranch. Their bossman has offered to bus in six hundred men. The head of the Oregon State Police says he'll bring in eight hundred if he has to. The FBI has already flown the SWAT team down from Seattle to link up with their Portland team."

My face conveyed my disbelief.

"Trust me, Nirgun," Rammurti said. "This isn't rumor, it's fact. I can't tell you how I know, but I know."

I told no one. I only half-believed him. How could I guess then that every word he spoke was true?

On October 1, 1985 at the evening press conference, a reporter asked Bhagwan a question that threw a monkey wrench into the gears of my life: "There's a rumor around that the National Guard is being mobilized, that you're going to be arrested tomorrow." Remembering Rammurti's story, I held my breath.

"If they arrest me I will enjoy it," Bhagwan answered. "These two hands handcuffed you have to show to the world. And with me five thousand sannyasins will voluntarily ask to be arrested."

"What if they say, 'No, we're not interested in arresting you?'"

"Then they will sit around the prison and fast there unto death. So America will know something new."

"Devaraj," I said the next day. "Did you hear what Bhagwan told the press last night? About all of us fasting if he were arrested?"

"Fasting?" Devaraj' cup of tea paused in midair, halfway between the table and his startled mouth.

"He said we would sit outside the prison and fast there unto death. I think it's a great idea."

"Fast unto death?" he chortled. "My dear Nirgun. A sannyasin's idea of a fast is the time between tea and dinner!"

Devaraj laughed at his own joke and I had to laugh with him. It was true. We both knew it.

Three weeks later Vivek burst into the kitchen. Her eyes were really wide, and flashing. I looked at her, startled. She was usually so cool.

"Nirgun!" Her voice showed her excitement. "Bugsy is going for a holiday. Can you help Nirupa pack?"

Going for a holiday? With all the rumors, and rumors of rumors?

"Where?" I managed, and she laughed. "I really don't know," she said. "Hasya has arranged it all."

"Can I come ?" I asked eagerly. Vivek flew across the kitchen and hugged me.

"There's only room for a few on the plane, Nirgie," she said, her eyes and voice soft. "But we'll all be together soon. I promise you!" She gave me a little shake and ran off down the corridor.

I watched from the kitchen window as the cars left for our airport, Bhagwan and Vivek in the first, Devaraj supervising the loading of baggage. They had just pulled away and Devaraj was piling bags into the second car with Chetana, Nirupa and Mukti when the telephone rang. It was a frantic Sukh, one of our lawyers, on the other end.

"Who is that? Nirgun, is it true that Bhagwan is planning to fly off the ranch?"

"He's already left," I told him, and heard his sharp intake of breath.

"Nirgun, can you stop him?" His voice was almost a shout." It's very important!"

Stop Bhagwan? The idea struck me as ludicrous. But the urgency in Sukh's voice—I dropped the phone, ran outside and yelled at Devaraj as he was getting into the second car.

"Raj! Sukh wants you to stop Bhagwan! Says it's urgent!"

I saw the laugh on his face as he threw out his hands in a gesture of impotence, got in the car and drove away.

I join a singing, weeping crowd of sannyasins at our airport. As Bhagwan's plane takes off I see the upturned, incredulous faces of reporters and police among the red throng. We watch together as the Lear jet sweeps upward and turns. Not west across the Pacific. Not north to Canada. Not south to Mexico. East. East, across three thousand miles of hostile territory.

I shut my eyes and see our master settled on the plane, eyes closed; settled inside himself. And I know that inside himself a great chuckle is happening. A risky game is getting riskier by the minute—but this time the rascal himself is carrying the ball. And, as it comes to pass, the chains. Into every living room in America.

Chapter 19

Hungry for Justice

ASHEESH WALKS INTO the kitchen while I am cleaning. There is a timeless quality to the morning, everything is taking longer than it usually does.

"Bhagwan has been arrested," he tells me, quietly. "In Charlotte, North Carolina."

I am not surprised. Not angry, not fearful. The news carries a sense of the inevitable, as if life is a drama unfolding and every event has its own logic, no more and no less important than rubbing the big glass jars till they sparkle like frosted grass in the morning sun.

Anger comes later.

All morning the vultures swarm the ranch. I count forty in Magdalena at lunch, their microphone beaks thrust out ready to suck the tears of disciples into electronic tubes to feed their avid audience.

Reporters dig frantically to fill the dead air time, the blank notebook. "Don't you feel abandoned?" "Resentful?" "Deserted?"

Bhagwan Shree Rajneesh under arrest in North Carolina, October 1985.

A sannyasin replies in a southern drawl, "Ah guess he's pulled the rug out from under us so often we've jes' gotten used to it."

The next night, house staff and gardeners gather in Lao Tzu living room to watch the late news. It's October 29, 1985. A disembodied voice erupts in the tense silence:

"This is *ABC News Nightline*, reporting from Washington; Ted Koppel. Joining us now from the Mecklenberg County Jail in Charlotte, North Carolina, is the Bhagwan Shree Rajneesh." The note of glee in his voice sends a shiver through my body.

Mukta hears it too. She sits rigid next to me, staring at the screen. Her thick tousled hair tumbles over her shoulders. Grief fills her wide brown eyes.

The camera zooms in on Bhagwan in a small bare room with barred windows. Dressed in prison green, he sits on a metal bench, a brown paper bag by his side. He answers Koppel's questions in a soft roar: "Without any arrest warrant I have been arrested, on the point of guns! I have not committed any crime! I am going to fight for the American Constitution against American politicians. They are prostituting democracy and the constitution both."

Bhagwan speaks with the same assurance as always. But inside me a cloud of foreboding swells. He takes life playfully, but the American authorities are deadly serious.

They mean him harm. I know it.

"Let's go down there, Nirgun," Mukta whispers. "I'll pay your way."

I seek out Padma, an artist and the commune's fashion designer since our old Poona days, and tell her I'm going to Charlotte with Mukta and Haridas.

Her eyes widen. "I thought we weren't supposed to go there," she interrupts, "so the Christians won't get upset."

"I know, but we're going anyway. Hasya's flown to Charlotte, Kaveesha's in charge now, and she's pretty mad at us. Padma, could you find me some sort of disguise? I want to stand in front of the jail as a kind of a symbol for everyone who can't be there."

She rummages in her cupboards and finds a floor-length red cape with enveloping hood and a pair of enormous sunglasses. She gives me a warm hug.

"What will you do about food while you're on the vigil, love?" she asks.

"Don't worry," I tell her. "I haven't eaten since the arrest. And you know," the words pop out, surprising me, "I just might not eat again as long as he's in jail."

On the plane we read the news that Sheela and several of her moms have been arrested in Germany. They've been living openly in a small village, Hausern, for almost two months, but were suddenly taken into custody ten hours after Bhagwan's arrest. The papers blazon the charges against Sheela: wire-tapping, arson, attempted murder—and the same columns cover the story of Bhagwan's arrest. Any reader would be confused and would connect Bhagwan with her crimes. It's October 31, and this feels like an ugly Halloween trick.

By 10 that morning Mukta, Haridas, and I are sitting in the courtroom in Charlotte, North Carolina.

Bhagwan walks slowly into the room, his chained hands held together in front of him. When he sees us, his smile lights up the whole dismal room. He returns the namaste of the sannyasins arrested with him: Vivek, Chetana, Nirupa, Mukti, Devaraj, and Jayesh, a land developer whose advice Bhagwan welcomes.

When Bhagwan is seated, Vivek gets up from her seat and goes to sit beside him. A guard tries to stop her and she brushes him aside. Throughout the hearing she sits beside Bhagwan, holding his hand.

Magistrate Barbara Delaney, a big brown-haired woman, enters, and the court rises. She sits down with her body averted from Bhagwan. Not once during the two-day bail hearing do I see her look at him.

The charges against Bhagwan are hardly the kind to deserve chains: entering the United States on a tourist visa when he really intended to stay, and encouraging marriages between his disciples that would allow non-Americans to live in Rajneeshpuram. The prosecutor tells the court that Bhagwan knew of these charges and was fleeing from arrest. They want him denied bail.

I prick up my ears when I hear Magistrate Delaney speak of "the arrest without warrants of, I think, 7 individuals, who are now before the court."

So there was no arrest warrant, just as Bhagwan had told Ted Koppel! I know a warrant isn't needed for an obviously criminal act, like a rape or murder in progress, but what is obviously criminal about flying from Oregon to North Carolina? The case should be dismissed on the spot!

Portland INS officer Joseph Greene tells the court that Bhagwan's immigration lawyer has tried to arrange with US Attorney Charles Turner, if an arrest were contemplated, to fly Bhagwan down to the Portland courthouse to surrender himself.

"Did Mr. Turner tell you his response?"

"Yes, Mr. Turner did. He said that it was not acceptable."

Now I know the reason for Bhagwan's 'flight'! If the US Attorney General in Portland had refused his offer to surrender peacefully in Portland, they must have been planning an arrest in the commune. Sannyasins would be aghast, angry. Even the tiniest incident, real or imagined, could become the flash point for a massacre. Bhagwan had averted the danger by flying off the ranch.

The prosecutor continues to question Greene, implying that Bhagwan is guilty of the crimes Sheela and several of her 'moms' have been charged with, which include attempted murder. He insists that Bhagwan is a public danger and should be held without bail.

Our American lawyer stands up, pale with anger.

"Your Honor," he says, "I think the only danger here is to the United States Constitution. This attorney general knows full well that the only reason why the people who attempted these alleged assassinations are in custody today is because my client, Bhagwan Shree Rajneesh, called for complete and total cooperation with law enforcement.

"The attempted murder is against one of these defendants!" He points to Devaraj. "And yet this attorney has the gall to come here and try to hoodwink this court into thinking that these defendants are involved in those murder attempts!"

The prosecution goes on to recite sensational stories that have been printed across the country about "The Bhagwan." The judge finally rules that these stories are not admissible as evidence, but not before avid reporters in the courtroom have scribbled down every lurid detail for tomorrow's headlines.

No witness, no document to prove Bhagwan's involvement in any crime is produced.

The chief prosecution witness, Joe Greene, admits that Bhagwan has complied with all US immigration rules and that if he were released today, he would not be facing deportation from the United States.

On the second day of the bail hearing Magistrate Delaney suggests that letting Bhagwan go back to Rajneeshpuram would be like letting Brer Rabbit back into the briar patch.

"Of course," she quips, "I know if I send the Bhagwan back to jail in Oregon I may have to put a restraining order on Sandy." Sandy, his Scottish jail nurse, has become so devoted even the judge knows about it.

Sagaresh, a witness for the defence, mounts the stand. A noted surgeon from Houston, he is a big man with a bush of white hair and dancing blue eyes. When the judge asks him if he doesn't regret the hundreds of thousands of dollars he has poured into Rajneesh coffers, he is quiet for a few seconds.

"How can I make you understand, Your Honor," he says, finally, "that if I gave Bhagwan everything I have, it would be nothing compared to what he has given me?"

Bhagwan's face is radiant as he looks at the doctor. I am infected by his radiance. A wave of delight swells up from below the belly button, melts the hard swollen lump of my heart. Not the froth of laughter, a wave of pure joy.

I know that everything is happening as it should. Our Brer Rabbit is safe in a briar patch of his own choosing. He chooses to speak with his own voice, and that voice has led him, relentlessly, here. To jail and shackles and public humiliation.

And it doesn't matter a bit. No one and no thing can touch his freedom, his joy. Or mine, or yours. That is his message to the world. That is why he is here, hogging the headlines.

Judge Delaney refuses bail and orders Bhagwan sent back to Oregon for trial.

She releases Chetana, Nirupa, and Mukti, and sets bail of $25,000 each for Devaraj, Vivek and Jayesh.

I don't stand when Delaney leaves the courtroom; she has not earned my respect. I rise only to namaste Bhagwan as he leaves, smiling.

Rain sluices down the next day as I stand in front of the jail. Green lawns stretch in front of the low brick building, softening its grim message. A guard comes out once and stares in my direction, then goes back inside. Bhagwan has sent word to those arrested with him that they should go back to the ranch.

Cars swish past. A maroon sedan stops, a woman runs over. She presses an umbrella into my hand without a word and runs back to her car. A man brings me a cup of coffee. Bhagwan has touched some hearts here in conservative Charlotte.

A TV van pulls up in front of me and a reporter gets out with his video camera. I dislike being photographed, always have.

"Could you tell me why you are standing here in the rain?" he asks.

"I'm protesting the arrest and shackling of an innocent, beautiful human being," I tell him.

"You are talking about Bhagwan Shree Rajneesh?"

"Yes," I say, with finality.

"Could you tell me your name, where you're from?" he persists.

"No," I answer. "I could be any one of thousands of his friends who want to be here and are staying away so as not to upset the people of Charlotte."

I turn away and he clicks off the camera.

I see the TV slice that night in my hotel room. Rain-drenched me in my Halloween getup, huge befogged glasses, long spindly hair straggling out from under the loose hood—not your usual TV glamor queen.

A keg of dynamite explodes. Mukta and Haridas storm into my hotel room. They lambaste me, lecture me, push me to drop my vigil.

Mukta scowls, disgust and anger plain on her unsmiling face. She has never been angry with me before in all the years we've worked together. "Why are you doing this, Nirgun?" she snaps. "We've been told not to stir things up around here. What good do you think it will do?"

"I don't honestly know, Mukta. But it can't do any harm. They've already refused bail."

"You are making an ass of yourself!" Haridas shouts. "This is nothing but a great ego trip you're on!"

"And why the hell aren't you eating?" storms Mukta, brown eyes flashing fire. "What is this, Nirgun?"

Shocked at their fury, I stammer, "I can only say it feels right to me, and I can't see that it's hurting anyone."

Unable to change my decision, they stalk out.

I'm in bed asleep that night when the phone rings. Long distance. "Nirgun!" Vivek's voice comes through, clear, sharp, authoritative. A voice I've never heard, it shakes me wide awake. "What's all this nonsense I've been hearing about you? Are you on some kind of hunger strike? You must return to the ranch at once!"

I try to explain that I'm only going to stay till Bhagwan leaves. My words fail to make a dint.

"Why are you doing this? It's just your ego, you know!" She goes on and on.

I tell her I'll look into it and hang up on her. The phone rings again but I don't answer. I phone down, tell the night clerk to hold any calls.

Sleep has vanished. I let my mind turn over, replaying what I've heard.

What if they are right, what if my ego has sneaked in and taken over, and my deep down feeling of rightness is just an illusion? How can I know? How can we ever know if we're following our own inner voice or the voice of ego? What in hell's half acre is this rain dance all about?

Suddenly I understand that I don't need to understand. Bhagwan's whole message is to listen to myself. No matter how absurd or difficult, follow my own still, small voice, making sure it harms no one. Get rid of the learned crap, the rational voice that drowns it out. Get rid of the gut urge-to-merge that keeps each one of us handcuffed to family, club, nation, church—to the commune!

"Be your own self. Leave the rest to existence."

He's said it all so often in so many ways. But it has taken a real-life device, his savage imprisonment, to drive the lesson into my blood and bones.

I snuggle into the pillows, close my eyes and drift to sleep.

Still standing in front of the jail two days later, I catch a tiny glimpse of a white figure entering a police car. I namaste. The guards are between us, Bhagwan can't see me, but it doesn't seem to matter.

Back in Portland I book into Hotel Rajneesh. The desk calendar reads November 5; I barely believe it. I've only been gone for six days.

My suitcase disappears, and through the window I see Haridas loading it onto the bus for the ranch. I take the suitcase off the bus, carry it to my room and lock the door.

An hour later I answer a knock. It's Hasya! She's Bhagwan's secretary now, she'll know what's happening! But her face is white, strained.

"Has Bhagwan come yet?" I ask, fearing the worst.

"No, he hasn't, Nirgun," she says. "We don't know where he is. Our lawyers are trying to find out." My heart plummets, I can think of nothing to say.

"I came to ask you to give up your vigil." Hasya puts her hand on my shoulder and looks in my eyes. Sad, stern. "It's very important that we all stay as low key as possible. The people in Oregon are hostile, and with Sheela's crimes I can't blame them. We can't rock the boat while Bhagwan is in jail."

"Just standing in front of the jail doesn't feel like rocking the boat," I tell her honestly. But her eyes flash.

"Nirgun, I'm asking you not to do it! For Bhagwan's sake!"

I don't answer. She turns and walks out.

How could it make matters worse for Bhagwan than they already are? As the full meaning of her words sinks in, sweat starts on the back of my neck. Charlotte to Portland: six hours of direct flying time has mysteriously expanded to more than twenty-four. He's in the custody of a government who hates everything he stands for. His whereabouts are unknown even to his lawyers. What is going on? What are they doing to him?

My hands reach out, unbidden, for the red cloak, the sunglasses.

Even though Bhagwan is not in the Portland jail, I continue my vigil. More heavy and cold than in Charlotte, the rain pours down.

The next night two of Hasya's top lieutenants come to my room. I pounce on them for news. "Has Bhagwan been found yet? Is he okay?"

The curly-haired woman grins uncertainly. "He's been found all right, thanks to the press. He's in a jail in Oklahoma. We're fighting to get him sent back here tomorrow."

A pregnant pause . . . They know I live in Bhagwan's house and it's obvious they don't like the job they've been handed. The woman tackles it first, her cheeks flushing, her eyes not meeting mine.

"Nirgun, Hasya says it's really important that you stop your vigil."

"She's already told me that," I say patiently. "And I've told her that it feels absolutely right to me."

"Hasya says if you don't stop, you'll have to leave the hotel."

Leave the hotel! I have less than ten dollars. Shades of Sheela! I shake my head.

"Why should I leave the hotel? It's my hotel as much as hers, and I'm disturbing no one."

"Do you have enough money if you have to leave here?" the man asks quietly. I know he will give me money if needed.

"I've got enough for a flophouse," I tell him. Then add, laughing, "After all, food isn't going to cost me a thing!"

They leave.

I sit down and write a note to Hasya, setting down the facts: That after I'd seen the TV shots of Bhagwan in jail, it came to me that I could not eat again until he was free; that hunger strikes can be effective—I cite the case of Sakharov, the Russian dissident; that I am tired of being hassled and will not talk to any more messengers.

I take the letter down, slip it in her message box. The kitchen staff conscript me to make oatmeal cookies.

The next day I sit from eight a.m. till six p.m. in the open park in front of the jail, in the heaviest rainstorm I've ever known. The clouds simply open and the rain sheets down. Charlotte was a trickle by comparison.

The city has taken on a festive note, but not a pleasant one. I think of Madame de Farge and her cronies knitting and cackling in front of the guillotine.

As the day wears on a feeling of dread settles in, an intuitive sense of danger that demands some kind of action, like a grouse dragging her wing across the hunter's path to draw his attention away from her hidden chicks. But here the hunter himself is hidden. Helplessness mingles with dread as I sit on in the rain. I remember another time when I waited, helpless and filled with dread, day after rainy day, for news of a loved one.

When I was 14 my father took his own life.

Dad didn't just believe, he **knew** he was more than his body. When he learned that he had a cancer the size of an orange in his stomach, he arranged to drown in a accident on the job so that mother would receive Workmen's Compensation.

I knew he was dreadfully ill, I'd seen him turn thin and grey over the summer. One day I came across him retching by the riverbank. I can see him still, on his knees on the silver sand, his body racked with dry, soundless convulsions. His back was to me; he didn't know I had come.

I left him there, without a word, without a touch, slipping off into the woods. Knowing with certainty that he had come out here to be alone. I lay in my cedar haven for hours, frozen into a space beyond thought, beyond feeling.

Two days later father lined us up formally on the stairs. He hugged the baby, shook hands with Arthur and Robin and me.

"Rosemary, you're the oldest girl at home now," he said. "Look after Mother." Then he left as if for a regular fish warden run, mother walking beside him, his arm around her waist. But her shoulders were shaking with enormous sobs. My eyes were dry, my mouth parched, my body turned to stone.

He was gone. The days ticked by. We pretended everything was normal, knowing he would want it so. On the fourth day mother sent me to the Indian village to ask if anyone had seen his boat. In front of a shack on the riverside Big Tom sat in the morning sun mending his fishing net. I asked, "Father? Boat? Did you see?"

His face turned a dull red. "Sorry," he said. He pointed down-stream. "Towing big boom, no can stop."

An endless pause. "Sorry, boat go around like this. . . ." Big Tom drew circles on the ground.

A great burst of pain filled my chest. His simple sketch in the dirt cut away all pretence, exposed the raw wound. Dad was really gone, and he wasn't coming back.

No tears came, only the suffocating pain.

We found the Robin L at the head of the inlet, still riding the waves, her engine dead. I sat in the stern of the neighbor's gasboat, staring down into the terrible frigid white-capped water. The cold crept up through my feet, through my body, to my heart.

We never did talk about Dad's death, Mother and I, except for one brief question and answer on my twenty-first birthday. I'd helped her settle in her own cozy home in Ladner—not grand but with lights and running water and lots of windowsills to put her hundred and twenty varieties of beans on to dry.

After she brought in the birthday cake and put it down on the table, Mother asked me, tears sliding down: "Rosemary, could I have stopped him? Should I?"

I could only hug her and say, "No, Mom, you couldn't. And you shouldn't."

Remembering, I wait outside the jail in Portland. There is nothing else to do. Bhagwan is still in Oklahoma.

That night Vivek comes to my room, eyes huge and dark in her white face. She is frantic with worry, desperate to get Bhagwan out of jail.

"Nirgun," she says softly, "Don't you think we should publicize your hunger strike? We gave the prosecutors a copy of your letter to Hasya, but they're not likely to make it public. I think we should tell the press. What's the good of a hunger strike if no one knows about it?"

Again that strange, total certainty. I put my arms around her, hug her gently. "Not yet, Vivecker," I say, using my pet name for her. I'd never said it out loud before. "Not unless they refuse bail here too."

Vivek steps back and looks at me, her face drawn in lines of despair, her voice almost a whisper as she tells me, "Our lawyers say there isn't a hope in hell of getting bail here."

Next morning in front of the jail I look at the facts. If Bhagwan isn't granted bail I will starve to death. Can I hang in there?

All through my life I've had flashes of being separate from my body. My childhood without mirrors created a sense of just-plain-being without a physical image to correspond to it. My out-of-body experience when pregnant and other timeless moments have left the unshakable sense that "I" am a separate entity.

Now the very act of depriving the body of food has increased this feeling of separateness. The thought of leaving it behind creates no flicker of fear. Ten days on a diet of water has left my body light, free, with no discomfort and no reason to expect any. Death in fact is beginning to look like just another adventure.

What about my kids?

A sudden stab of pain shatters my calm reckoning. Saguna will understand, he'll be right there with me. Blair will understand a little, he's a seeker at heart. But Craig hates Bhagwan with a fierce and wondrous hatred. The thought of his rage and horror, finding his skin-and-bones mother . . . They'll have to phone him. His name is in my passport. Tears stream down just imagining his face, his anger and pain are so clear to me.

But behind the tears some part of me is standing back, witnessing them. Witnessing my certainty.

I can't chain myself to family, to my children, the sweetest bondage of all. I am alone and must remain alone. I have known the bitter-sweet taste of aloneness. The sugar-sweet urge-to-merge will pull me away from my own inner wisdom, smother my inner voice. That has been the lesson of the ranch. That has been the lesson of my life.

The tears fade.

The certainty stays.

That afternoon reporters shout to each other. Bhagwan has been brought into the Portland jail by the back door! At six o'clock I run all the way to the hotel. The lobby is filled with weeping, laughing sannyasins.

After visiting Bhagwan in jail, Hasya comes again. Her voice and manner are soft, but she brings out her biggest weapon.

"Bhagwan has sent a message for you, Nirgun," she says, and I hold my breath, delighted: Bhagwan will understand. "He says you are to stop your hunger strike."

For a split second my heart seems to stop beating. I stay silent, puzzled. How can Bhagwan tell me such a thing when I'm doing what comes naturally—not from my mind, not from my feelings, but from a silent space I've met with oh-so-rarely in my long life. "Did he say why?"

"He says he doesn't want any of his sannyasins suffering because of him."

A great wave of relief floods through me, brings a grin to my face. "Tell Bhagwan," I say, laughing, "that I'm not suffering, not at all. Just doing my own thing."

Hasya looks at me, her thin eyebrows lifting. How can I explain it to her? To myself? An ancient Buddhist saying comes to me. Quoted often in Zen stories, interpreted in many ways, to me it means Don't allow even the voice of the master to drown out your own inner voice.

"Remember?" I tell Hasya. "'If you meet the Buddha on your path, kill him.'"

Hasya stares at me for a long moment. Then she turns silently and leaves. She doesn't come again.

In the morning I squeeze into the white, oak-panelled courtroom. Officials open the jury box to make room for the crowd clamoring at the door.

At ten o'clock Bhagwan is ushered in. He wears a favorite green robe and knitted hat to match. I am elated to see that he is not hand-cuffed. During the hearing he sits totally still, dwarfed by his big, burly lawyer. He speaks only once, to answer the judge: "Not Guilty."

I look at Judge Edward Leavy for clues, but his long wrinkled face, topped by horn-rimmed glasses under careful white hair, is un-readable.

Prosecutor Weaver again alleges Bhagwan's involvement in Sheela's crime of salmonella poisoning and her plans to assassinate government officials, and alleges also his involvement in illegal weapons on the ranch. Defense attorney Brian O'Neill cross-examines the prosecution witness, Joseph Greene.

"Is it not true that it was Bhagwan who told the authorities about Sheela's crimes and invited them to investigate?"

"Yes," Greene replies.

"And was it not a witness provided by Bhagwan's lawyers that gave the testimony about salmonella poisoning?"

"Yes, it was."

"And with respect to the weapons on the ranch, your own investigation disclosed the fact that every one was appropriately registered?"

"Yes," Greene admits.

Each side summarizes its position.

Then in a measured, questioning tone Judge Leavy asks about the finances of the defence.

Waves of delight shiver down my spine. Sweet Jesus! He's talking money! He's going to let Bhagwan out on bail! I see the face of our sannyasin lawyer, Niren: blank, wide-eyed with shock.

The judge sets bail at $500,000. Bhagwan is free.

My body relaxes like a cat in front of a glowing fire, my mind fills with just one ecstatic thought: "Now I don't have to go out in that fucking rain again!"

Peacocks are preening in the late fall sun outside the window as I wash up pots in Lao Tzu kitchen. Centuries have passed since I left for Charlotte; in fact it is only two weeks. Bhagwan has been welcomed back with a madly joyous celebration and is safe in his room down the corridor; ranch business goes on as usual. Nothing has changed. Everything has changed.

I make oatmeal cookies for tea. I eat slowly, gratefully with Chetana, Mukti, Nirupa; we are suspended in time, waiting for Bhagwan's trial. After the miracle of the bail hearing, anything seems possible.

In the evening Vivek brings up Bhagwan's thali and puts it down on the counter. "Nirgun"—her voice is low, she is keeping it steady by effort. "Bhagwan is going to be leaving. You and Mukti need to pack up the kitchen."

I look at her blankly. "What about the trial?"

"Our lawyers have agreed to a bargain with the government," she says grimly. "They'll let him leave the country if he'll plead guilty to a couple of crimes."

"But he's innocent!" I explode. "They don't have *any* evidence! How can they ask him to plead guilty?"

"I know that and you know that, but we can't take the chance of his going to jail. He can make a special plea, saying that he's innocent but is willing to plead guilty because of the danger to himself and the rest of us."

"But what could they find to charge him with?"

"They say he encouraged marriages that would help non-Americans to stay in the country. And that he told a lie on his visa application—said he was just visiting when he really meant to stay. Our lawyers say those charges are hardly ever prosecuted in America. If people admit guilt the fine is only twenty-five dollars!"

I burst out laughing. Federal, state and county police and a dozen government departments have pulled out all stops for years. The media has blazoned accusations of murder, fraud, and conspiracy. And all they can come up with are these innocuous charges—like a fisherman who puts out a million-dollar seine net and brings up a single herring.

Two days later at Portland airport we cluster near the waiting jet, singing, dancing, whooping it up. Vivek, Devaraj, Chetana, Nirupa, Mukti and Hasya are already on the plane.

We hear him long before the burgundy Rolls comes in sight: the scream of sirens, the snarling roar of a pack of motorcycles. An escort of fifty police sweeps down in tandem, weaving in and out. Their black suits, helmets, and goggles, their giant machines make them look like monsters from outer space. I watch with strange elation as the presidential escort roars to a stop.

The Rolls drives onto the tarmac. We fall silent as Bhagwan steps out. Palms together, he greets us slowly, looking at each in turn.

I watch him climb the steps of the plane. Midway he stops and turns to wave, his long beard silvery grey against his dark robe. Smiling. Turning again in the doorway, twinkling with silent laughter. Signing with his long fingers a "V" for victory.

Chapter 20
Meditation Madness

*E*ARLY NOVEMBER, shining-sun-and-blue-sky November in Poona.
It's two years since the Oregon commune dissolved into thin air.
I join a river of sannyasins flowing into the vastness of Buddha
Hall. Bhagwan is well again after a seven-week illness and I'll see him
tonight! Frightening reports have come through on the sannyas grapevine in these past two years. As I wait in the silent hall, a ticker tape in
my head clicks over, counting off the events of his world tour. . . .

> violently arrested and deported from Crete . . . denied permission to
> sleep in lounge of Heathrow Airport while pilots rest, forced to spend
> night in the airport jail . . . barred from Germany by order of parlia-
> ment . . . deported from Uruguay . . . denied permission to refuel in
> Canada . . . forced out of Lisbon by police, pressured to return to
> India . . . harassed by police in his bedroom in Poona . . . threatened
> by armed Hindu fanatics . . . recently struck by mysterious illnes . . .

The silence in Buddha Hall deepens, the stillness is absolute. I
hear the sound of a car approaching. Unseen musicians play a soft

melody, a door opens—and he is here, walking up to the podium with his small, careful steps: magnificent in a robe of shining patterned white that twinkles as he moves. A bold black panel surges down the front, a black hat glitters with sequins.

Bhagwan pauses on the podium to namaste us before sitting down. His luminous dark eyes look direct into mine for a timeless moment. The old rush of contentment fills me along with a ripple of sadness. His eyes hold no hint of a twinkle, his beard is snow white.

"My beloved ones," he says softly, "I have been away from you much too long." Sadness swells as he describes the details of his mysterious illness: a simple ear infection that would not heal, weight loss, hair loss, tingling, sleeplessness, bone pain, nausea. Doctors suggest one probable cause: poisoning. "I have been poisoned by Ronald Reagan's American government."

Bhagwan describes his midnight arrival at an Oklahoma jail; the attempt to sign him in under a false name; the strange food served at five in the morning, the unconsciousness afterward. His doctors have sought out expert opinion on poisons that work slowly and leave no trace in the body.

I am overwhelmed by a sense of the inevitable. Others are crying openly, but for me no tears come. A tide of surrender flows inwards, into every cell of my body: *Existence has its own ways.* Inside I hear his words from another time, another place: "There is going to be no death. My body will disappear, your body will disappear. That will not make any change."

Our connection is beyond time and space. I have had glimpses of this truth before; now it goes deep inside. I look at him—not listening to his words, just drinking in his exquisite beauty and grace, the eloquent gestures of his long fingers, the flash of his fiery eyes. *Existence has its own ways, and yet* . . . I want to gaze at *this* body/form, *this* grace, *this* beauty, here, now and forever.

After discourse I walked a mile to a telephone station and phoned Saguna in West Australia.

Our letters had been infrequent and skating on the surface, but now on the phone I told him straight out, "Saguna, Bhagwan has just told us he was given slow poison by the American government. I thought you'd want to know."

There was silence at the other end of the line.

Finally he asked, "How is he, Mom?"

"I don't know. How can you ever tell with him? It seems to be an effort for him to talk, and that's so unlike him."

Another silence, and then he spoke slowly. "Well, I guess Elli and I better have another look at our plans."

I took the bull by the horns. "What's with you, Saguna?" I asked. "Are you still feeling bruised by the ranch? "

Thousands of miles away I heard him take a deep breath.

"Well, I guess the answer is po: yes and no. It's like . . . Poona was a sort of a quest, a mysterious, spiritual quest. *You* know, Mom, you were there. And then on the ranch, I really had to change gears there. All of a sudden there was this challenge and excitement, 'Got a city to build' kind of energy."

Another long pause. I had to bite my mother-tongue to keep from interrupting.

"There was this big feeling of accomplishment. And then it turned out to be an illusion. That was a major letdown for a lot of us." I heard a trace of the old bitterness in his voice.

"Then suddenly I'm back out in the world again after eight years. Now it's about finding home base and cash flow. There's a kind of feeling of power and security in being able to buy things. . . ."

His voice trailed away, then came back. "And you know, Mom, now some of the people coming back from Poona seem to me almost like fanatics sometimes, like addicts who can't be happy without that magic fix. I mean, 'If you can't make it happen on your own then it ain't real, babe,' you know?"

What could I say to that?

"Saguna, I do know. I know sannyasins who seem to do that, seem to rely on something outside to solve their problems. But that's *their* problem, not yours or mine. The reason I called was to let you know that if you do want to see Bhagwan again, there might not be a lot of time left."

"Yeah. I get the picture. I'm glad you called to tell me. And Mom," the old soft tone was back in his voice, "maybe you'll be seeing me sooner than you think."

I hung up and paid the huge bill without gasping, filled only with delight that we'd been able to talk heart-to-heart again.

Walking home I remembered how the two years away from

Bhagwan had been for me. When he flew out of America for points unknown, in a small plane, only essential personal staff could go with him. Since Mukti was cooking for him now, my presence wasn't critical and I didn't even ask. Suddenly the urge to see my sons again had risen up, loud and strong. Arup's mother gave me the airfare home.

I flew straight to see Blair, not knowing how he would greet me. Since the black day when he returned the $100 I sent, in unguarded moments my mind had stormed with self-reproach. Why didn't I go to him? I loved him with a fierce mother's love, a love known to be the strongest bond in nature. Yet the need to follow my own inner voice had proved stronger.

An intense religious experience had brought Blair to embrace Christ. I found him caretaking an ancient nonprofit apartment building. He greeted me quietly, but I sensed he had forgiven me, was glad to see me. The loss of his kids—he refused visiting privileges, not wanting them to be torn apart—had driven him to spend years on the road, in agony of spirit and abject poverty. It seemed to have aged him, taken away the bright animated son I knew. But when he played at night with a four-piece band, all his old verve came back. Music had always been the center of his life, and now his saxophone, his flute, his clarinet had a richness I'd never heard before.

Other members of the band lived in the same building; day and night the high halls echoed as they practiced for their gigs. I brightened his room with paint and plants and cooked meals for the band, loving their music, their camaraderie. Just being with Blair, getting to know him, felt like such a blessing. I stayed four months.

"You can have both worlds together," Bhagwan had told me, "love and meditation, being with people, relating, and being alone." I relaxed into the sweetest relating of all: with my kids.

I visited Craig, now an executive in the computer department of a huge pulp and paper mill. Conferences at the best hotels, generous expense accounts, refresher courses in New York—he was enjoying the lifestyle I'd opted out of. Karen rejoiced in her huge garden, Tina and Kevin, now seven and five, were as lively as my own three had been. A snug nest—I could have stayed on. But I didn't want a nest.

Back once more in Vancouver, I answered an ad by a small social agency; refused a supervisory position and took on a loosely-defined job in a 16-room residence for ex-psychiatric patients.

The ranch had hit me between my social worker eyes. During Share-a-Home, I'd seen many "down-and-outers" come to life. They'd had no counseling, just worked and played in a friendly, open, active place where five thousand people (excluding Sheela and a dozen or so of her aides) had shared and shared alike. The difference between giving to the poor and breaking bread with friends engraved itself on my innards.

Now the mental health job got bent at the edges and shaped into something quite different. I locked up the files, pushed the interviewing desk into a corner, and forgot about "cases," "clients," "diagnosis," "prognosis." Don and I washed his walls while he sang in his rich baritone. Marie read her haikus to me while I polished the windows. Betty taught me to swim the breast stroke. Elena and I laughed and cooked great dinners for the whole crew once a week. We putted on the back lawn, picnicked on the beaches.

In those two years not one of the sixteen residents went back to a psychiatric ward. The agency director came, saw, marvelled, and booked a leave of absence to visit the commune.

After my pension kicked in, regulations required that I live in Canada six months of the year. I spent the other six in Poona, every year for the next eight years.

It never occurred to me to ask about working in LaoTzu again. While I'd been in the West existence had closed that door, just as ten years before the kitchen door had closed behind Neera with her tennis elbow and I'd stepped into her place.

Mukta gave me the gardens around Buddha Hall to care for. I reveled in the old familiar creak of bamboos, the slithering mongoose, the squawk of peacocks flying to roost in the trees, the burble of running streams around our open meditation hall.

The bamboos and delicate feathery tamarinds I'd helped to plant were now a shady jungle, thirty, forty feet tall. Neither flowers nor weeds could compete with them, and my main job was to keep the jungle incessantly watered, while listening to the music of the meditations. Every day the hose was left to dribble while I whirled, leaped, and shook in Nataraj and Kundalini.

In April of 1988 Bhagwan announced a new meditative therapy: "the most essential and fundamental one. It can take over the whole world."

The Mystic Rose meditation was devastatingly simple: laughing, crying, sitting—one week of each, three hours a day.

"The first part removes everything that hinders your laughter—all the inhibitions of past humanity, all the repressions. It brings a new space within you," he told us. "You have suppressed so much sadness, so much despair, so much anxiety, so many tears. They are all there, covering you and destroying your beauty, your grace, your joy. Tears will take out all the agony that is hidden inside you and laughter will take all that is preventing your ecstasy."

I sign up for the first Mystic Rose group. More than fifty of us crowd into a bare underground room with cream colored walls and a beige linoleum floor covered with single mattresses.

I laugh my way through the first week, zany spontaneous laughter for no reason at all. It wells up unbidden in great waves, minute after minute, hour after hour. My belly aches with it. The woman on the next mattress is lean and gangly with a wide, humorous mouth and fine long blonde hair that flies and straggles like mine. To look at her is to laugh. We trigger each other, rolling on the floor, hugging, wrestling, gasping.

On the first day of the second week a young helper with curly black hair puts a box of tissues beside each mattress. I smother laughter at the sight of it. Soon all around me people are snuffling, blowing, roaring out their grief. Try as I may tears will not come. I think of sad losses—Rover, father, Glen—all seem far removed, as if they had happened to someone else. I squeeze my eyes shut; pinch myself; make crying sounds to dredge up tears. Nothing. I am an outsider, adrift on a sea of misery.

The fourth day I give in to my keep-a-stiff-upper-lip British training and simply lie there, eyes closed. A soft arm touches my arm, a sobbing, tear-wet face is next to mine on the pillow. It is the black-haired girl. She says nothing, just lies there crying as if her heart would break.

Just her touch, and I am part of the whole quivering, crying jumble of bodies. Sadness overwhelms me, tears start to flow. Tears without cause, from a lifetime of hurting. I am part of a foundering, floundering humanity wondering why? Why? Why so much anguish, so much suffering, such rare flashes of joy?

The third week is called the Watcher on the Hill. It is held in a long corridor with a window wall facing out over the lush gardens of Lao Tzu. Each one of us sits alone, unconnected to the other. Silence comes on its own, without effort. I watch hour after hour, day after day as the heart slows, and the breath; and thoughts. Watch as they slow more and more, seem to stop for timeless moments.

This detachment came in handy one morning when I arrived in the garden to find fifty people kneeling in front of huge wet brightly colored messy papers on enormous boards. They were painting the plants around Buddha Hall. Brilliant, vivid, staining inks ran in little rivulets off sheets of plastic onto the white driveway; even worse, I saw one would-be painter dump her dirty paint water into the garden. Alarm bells rang in my head: Indian paint is really toxic.

Mukta had warned me about Meera's painting group, Chaos and Bliss, but I hadn't expected this much chaos.

I set off in search of Meera. Wild, alive, Japanese, her long black hair streaming down her back, she was kneeling in front of a painting holding an enormous brush while fifteen people watched breathlessly.

"Is easy to break old pattern," she said. "Is simple. I show you."

She dipped the brush in water and dragged it over the painting. The owner of the painting gasped. Meera started mopping up the surface with a sponge while color ran everywhere.

"Now painting can breathe," she said.

I stared, spellbound. I knew Bhagwan had chosen Meera to paint the covers for his books. Now as I watched the wild energy with which she worked, I understood why.

"Just let go," she said. "Let plants guide you. Let plants show you how to paint them."

The plants can't show you if you're killing them, I thought, laughing, as she got to her feet.

"Meera," I said, "Some people are throwing their painting water away in the garden."

Meera sighed. "Okay. We tell them again. Assistants tell them again. Every year this happen. Every year."

She raised her voice. "Assistants!" she called out.

Three people dropped their brushes and came at her call. Suddenly I recognized Amiyo, the fiery red-haired doctor I'd known on the ranch. Green paint was smeared on her face and her hands were bright blue.

"Careful," she laughed as she fell into my arms, holding her colorful palms away from my back.

"I didn't know you painted," I said, as soon as Meera finished instructing them about the dirty water.

"I didn't either," glowed Amiyo. "Six months ago I hadn't painted since high school. Last year I did one of Meera's groups and something just exploded in me."

I believed her. Her painting, a bold and colorful pattern of natural shapes, radiated joy, and so did she. I watched her show the painters where to dump their water. We helped them finish in time to eat and shower before discourse, hurrying, not wanting to miss by being late.

Today would be extra special: For the first time in nearly twenty years, a meditation was to be led by Bhagwan himself. And every meditation began with jokes, the more outrageous the better; sannyasins all over the world searched them out, sent them in.

Eyes laughing, Bhagwan picks up a pad from the table beside him and begins to read.

> Old man Chester Cheese, aged eighty-five, goes to a sperm bank to make a deposit. The young woman at the reception desk is skeptical. "Are you sure that you want to do this?" she asks.
>
> "Yes," says old Chester. "I feel it is my duty to give something from myself to the world."
>
> The woman gives him the jar and directs him to a room down the hall. When thirty minutes have passed and he does not return, the woman begins to worry that he might have had a heart attack. But just then the old man comes out of the room and approaches her.
>
> "Listen," he says, "I tried it with one hand, then I tried it with two hands; then I got it up and hit it on the sink; then I ran warm water on it, then cold water over it—and I still can't get the lid of the jar open!"

The hall rocks with laughter—not just at the joke, but because it is being told by a spiritual master. When the laughing dies away, Bhagwan tells another.

> Dr. Bones and Dr. Skinner are out duck hunting early one morn-

ing while it is still dark. They hear an owl in the tree above them snoring.

"I'm such a great surgeon," brags Bones, "that I can go up there and take out that owl's tonsils without even waking him up."

Ten minutes later Bones climbs down the tree and holds up two tiny tonsils.

"That's nothing," says Skinner, "I'm so nimble with my hands I'll climb up there and remove that owl's testicles without him feeling a thing!"

Sure enough, a few minutes later Dr. Skinner returns with a pair of tiny balls.

Months later the owl flies over the same tree with a friend.

"Hey!" says the friend, "It's bedtime. Let's sleep in that tree tonight."

"No thanks!" replies the owl. "I slept there a few months ago and ever since I haven't been able to hoot worth a fuck or fuck worth a hoot!"

After the laughter comes gibberish: to throw our craziness out, to break up the mind's fixation on words, words, words.

Bhagwan signals to our drummer, Nivedano. At the single beat of his drum the immense hall explodes as thousands of people pummel the air with their arms, scream and shout out nonsense sounds. I roar and giggle, jibber and snort and yell.

Bhagwan speaks. "Nivedano." A sudden drumbeat, sudden silence.

"Be silent.
  Close your eyes.
  Feel your body to be completely frozen.
  Now look inwards with your total life energy,
  with your total consciousness,
  and with an urgency as if this
  is going to be the last moment of your life."

A shaft of energy stabs from the top of my head to my navel— pressing, painful, pulling my attention from the silent world around to the silence inside.

"Only with urgency can you reach

> to the centre of your being,
> and at the centre of your being
> You are the Buddha."

His words wash over me, impelling, compelling, like the surge of a Big One carrying me in on its crest.

Another drumbeat. "Relax."

Bodies collapse like pricked balloons. We fold one into the others, joined together like the bumpy colored patches in an old-fashioned eiderdown. Utterly still.

> "Just watch.
> The body is not you,
> the mind is not you,
> you are only the witnessing.
> This experience of witnessing
> is the ultimate truth of your being."

My body sprawls, listening from the centre; falling into a relaxation so deep I barely hear him. His words drift to me like white clouds across a vast inner sky.

"Nivedano." A drumbeat.

> "Come back,
> but bring the buddha with you.
> Show the buddha in every action. . . .
> Show the beauty and the grace and the music."

I come back in time to respond to his long, careful namaste. Then he is gone. The music builds to repeated crescendos of sound. I sit still, eyes closed, more aware of the quiet place inside than of the wild celebration around me; slowly coming out, joining in the festive dance.

Chapter 21

Osho

*F*ROM THE SILENT MAGIC of Let Go meditation Bhagwan catapulted the commune into a storm of confusion. After a seven-week absence from Buddha Hall in December of 1988, he announced in discourse that Gautama the Buddha had entered his body, and that this had been verified by the seeress of one of the most ancient Shinto shrines in Japan. Twenty-five centuries ago Buddha had prophesied, "When I come again, I will have to take shelter in a man of similar consciousness."

I snorted inwardly. This gambit, coming from a master who stressed using our intelligence, reeked of yet another device.

"From now onwards I am Gautama the Buddha. You can call me the Beloved Friend. Drop the word 'Bhagwan' completely."

I heard a chorus of startled gasps, quickly stifled, and felt a tug at my own heart. *Not call him Bhagwan?*

'Bhagwan' means 'God' to the Hindus. Now he explained, "I have been calling myself Bhagwan just as a challenge to this country, to the

Christians, to the Mohammedans, to the Hindus."

To me the name connoted simple reverence, but he went on to hack my fond sentiment to shreds.

"The word 'bhagwan' is a very ugly word; *bhag* in Hindi is the male genitalia, *wan* is the female. I hate the word! I don't want to be called Bhagwan ever again. Enough is enough! The joke is over!"

This outrageous declaration threw the entire commune into a frenzy of speculation.

"What do you say?" asked Amiyo as we nabbed a table in the canteen after discourse. "Do you really think Buddha is in Bhagwan's body?"

"He's not called Bhagwan anymore," I muttered, not wanting to start an argument with her. But she persisted.

"Oh, right, whatever. But do you think it's true? Is Buddha really there?"

"Nah, it's just a device," drawled Sarlo. "He's pulled my leg so many times that now my left is a foot longer than my right."

"I don't know. I just don't know," said D.C. "Something's happened, something's changed. He's not the same."

"Oh, come on," I said. "The whole thing is hilarious, it's a spoof on reincarnation. He's just a rascal, period."

"But what if Buddha really is there?" insisted Amiyo.

"Come off it!" I snapped. "You're so beguiled by all this esoteric nonsense!"

They looked at each other. My impatience with esoteric conversations was well-known.

"But I thought enlightened people just melted into existence," persisted Amiyo. "I thought that was the whole point—that they didn't come back."

"Look, you two," I said with finality. "He's told us again and again not to pay attention to his words, just listen to him as we listen to the wind in the trees."

That silenced them for the moment, but when I left the table I looked back: they were at it again, head to head in animated speculation.

They weren't the only ones. Speculative gossip raged like wildfire as our Beloved Friend milked the joke, changing his name to Maitreya the Buddha, then announcing that the Buddha was unable to adjust to the twentieth century and had taken off. We could now call him Shree Rajneesh, Zorba the Buddha, or Buddha. A week later he fixed on Shree Rajneesh; two months later, Osho Rajneesh. Finally he became just plain Osho, a generic term in the Zen tradition meaning Beloved Master.

"How'd you like what's-his-name's discourse tonight?" asked Sarlo one evening as he slid his tray onto the table. "Keeping up with the Name of the Month Club?"

"It's hilarious, isn't it?" I said. "Maybe 'Osho' won't stick either, maybe he'll drop it tomorrow. With him nothing stays static."

"Boy, that's for sure," Amiyo laughed through a mouthful. "They're going crazy over in publications. I have a friend who works there. With every name change they're asking: do we republish everything with the new name? They don't know what they're supposed to be doing."

"Yup. He keeps pulling the rug out from under us," chuckled Sarlo. "First the leg, then the rug." A few seconds later he laughed out loud. "Osho is *big-time* Zen. Remember the Zen master who threw a disciple out the window, jumped on his chest and shouted 'Got it?' I bet Osho is the first master who ever threw his whole commune out the window!" We all roared at that one.

Only a week after our lighthearted table talk, Osho ended his discourse with the words: " Remember that *you* are a Buddha: *sammasati*."

Next day his new secretary Anando, an Australian lawyer, told us he wouldn't be speaking to us again, but would come out intermittently to sit with us in silence.

Osho began to give guidelines for the commune in the years to come. All the buildings were to be black, all windows of blue glass. He designed huge pyramids to be set in the midst of the ashram gardens.

A group he called the Inner Circle was to reach decisions about the continued functioning and expansion of the commune and his work. He chose twenty-one members and stressed that the inner workings of the committee were to remain a secret. The committee was not to be involved in spiritual matters.

"It is not a club to discuss philosophy," Anando reported. "It is a pragmatic and practical way to decide things."

Osho included a most unusual stipulation. All decisions of the Inner Circle must be unanimous! I shook my head when I heard it. No voting, no behind-the-scenes finagling to get votes: Could such a far-out idea possibly work?

I scrutinized the list and shook my head again. There were Devaraj* and Devageet, Chetana* and Mukta, Arup* and Anando, Jayesh and three members of the Hollywood set: Hasya, Kaveesha and John. Each one was a strong individual, and their backgrounds were as different as the world offers. If they could be unanimous, it would be a miracle.

Osho appointed Jayesh as chairman. I've always had a soft spot for Jayesh. Perhaps it's because he's a fellow Canadian, or because he plunged so absurdly from playing polo in Palm Springs to serving an infamous master in the Oregon desert. Or perhaps because he sparked the miraculous translation of Osho's vision into bold reality, all in six short years.

Jayesh is a very private person who hates to speak in public and gives no interviews to the press. But once when he talked to me in one of the new bright offices, relaxed in simple cream tunic and pants, a 10-minute scheduled interview expanded to more than an hour. He told me stories of his pre-Osho years with the Arica Institute in America, and how its founder, Oscar Ichazo, fully supported his sudden urge to join Rajneesh.

At one point Jayesh drifted into telling me an anecdote I'll remember always.

"One day I went to report to Osho—we were building the pyramids and I was telling him about some problem on the job. And he suddenly asked me, 'And how did that feel, Jayesh?'

"I was surprised, he never interrupts. I told him 'It wasn't anything much, just some minor business, Osho.' And he asked me again. 'And how did it feel, Jayesh?'

"Suddenly this great wave of anger flooded through me. I felt the blood rush into my face, I couldn't move or speak. And right then Osho said, '*That's* your ego, Jayesh.'"

Jayesh paused for a long moment, looking out the window. "I couldn't go back to work, Nirgun, I had to get away. For three days I stayed in a hotel in Bombay, running a fever."

---

* Osho gave these three disciples new names: Devaraj became Amrito, Chetana became Shunyo, and Arup became Garimo. To avoid confusion, the old names are kept in the remaining pages.

Jayesh on left, with his brother Yogendra and girlfriend Mayoori.

For me the story is an intimate glimpse of a master at work. Osho had risked offending a hard-working disciple in order to help him see the insidious ways of the ego, see and feel the anger that arises when our power, our authority is questioned.

And Jayesh, unlike Sheela, got the point. (Sheela, along with several of her moms, was now in jail, serving a five year sentence for salmonella poisoning, wiretapping and bombing: her urge to power had gone berserk.)

Osho asked for a rush job on his new bedroom, and the work hurried to completion. Sections of imported Italian marble, white streaked with dark grey, were cut so cunningly that each section appeared as an evocative abstract painting. Six dark blue glass panels separated the "paintings," each one reflecting an enormous crystal chandelier, bathing the room in sparkling, subdued light.

Seeing the room one day, weeks before its completion, I knew it at once for what it was. Osho had designed his own samadhi: an exquisite vault for the ashes that in India are called flowers.

I felt no shock, no sadness. To me his life was unfolding like this amazing room: serene, light, with a strange and powerful design.

Osho moved into this glorious space for two weeks, then moved back to his old room.

In August he hit us with another thunderbolt: We were all to wear the same colors again. When the ranch was ending, he had suggested for our own protection that we drop red and the mala. Now we were all to wear maroon in the commune during the day, black with white belts for therapists and group leaders, white to meet with him in the evening.

The robe meditation turned into a crazy monsoon dance. Entering the commune, sodden with rain and spattered with mud, we had to change into clean robes without lockers or proper changing rooms.

"Boy, you have to be alert around here," laughed Amiyo as we struggled to change in a tiny makeshift closet. "A friend of mine pulled her dress over her head the other day and bam! when she turned around her maroon robe was gone! Poof! Vanished!"

I must have looked skeptical.

"Really, it's true. The Poona tailors can't keep up to us. Suddenly we need four thousand maroon robes and four thousand white ones. No, eight thousand of each, because we have to wash them."

"Only Osho would introduce white just when the roads are drowning in mud," I said wryly. For me it was another test of our Irritability Quotient.

"Sure. I think the point of this whole thing is to get us to change our clothes with awareness." Amiyo suddenly shrieked with laughter. "Jesus, I just remembered what happened last night. This woman roars in through the front gate at six thirty-five, with five minutes to change into her white robe before they close the entrance to Buddha Hall. That's not enough time to make it to the changing place and back. So what does she do? She just throws down her pack and starts ripping her clothes off right there, right in front of everybody. The guard is telling her that this is not okay, and she doesn't even stop to argue with him. She just pulls off her dress while the Indians stand there with their eyes popping out, throws on her white robe, and walks into Buddha Hall. Now that's determination!"

I could understand her determination. Nothing could keep me from the White Robe Brotherhood, the meditation Osho told us was "the highest point of your whole day in the commune"—his final, most powerful meditation.

"White is the color of silence," he said once, and total silence fell with our first step into the exotic space of Buddha Hall. A hall without walls. Ethereal blue-green mosquito netting, held taut by slender curved metal poles, now enfolds a vast expanse of gleaming white marble floor leading to a green marble wall and podium. No posts interrupt the openness; the high oval ceiling appears to float in space. Heavy-crossed drapes, in a blue-green taffeta-like fabric, rustle when touched, so that every individual entering creates his own tiny explosion.

Promptly at seven Bhagwan came and led us in wild body movements for ten minutes, to music he devised after much experiment—wild, wordless music. At first the music and his equally wild conducting set off frenzied screams, till he sent out a message: "No screaming, this is not a football match." The more total our celebration, he told us through Anando, the deeper our meditation would go.

Music erupts in the packed hall. On the instant thousands of white-robed bodies go wild, dancing on the spot with thrusting arms and gyrating torsos, leaping/twisting/bending in delirious response to a frenzy of flute, violin, percussion.

Human energy rises in great crescendos of movement and music. Without words. Keeping the energy in, letting it build.

Trickles of sweat run down my cheeks, neck, back. The noisy pumping of my heart drowns out thought. I dance as one possessed. I am possessed, we all are. Possessed by love of this radiant human being. Possessed by his vision, that we are not solid bodies and static minds but one vast streaming energy that can take us to a space beyond the mind.

Three drumbeats, then silence. Indian music—the flute, the sitar, with long gaps of nothingness—enhances the silence. My body congeals into a stone statue, rivulets of sweat pouring down. Inside tiny rushes of energy charge about, contorting my face and hands. A driving shaft of the stuff stabs from navel to forehead, pounding on the third eye, pinning me in the present.

One night after White Robe I impulsively phoned Saguna again.

"It's incredible," I told him, "like an energy darshan for five thousand people."

"How's he doing, Mom? How's his health?"

"Well, on the one hand he seems so frail and on the other his energy is out of this world." I didn't know how to get across my sense of urgency without pulling a mother-interference number. "Do you think you'll be coming soon? How does it look?"

Vivek with Osho.

"Well, the life of a householder seems to be coming to a climax—an anticlimax, more like. You'll be glad to know that Elli and I have got over our trip with new toys. " He laughed, sadly. "Three years of constant busyness, telling myself that I'll relax and start meditating again 'as soon as,' and lately I've seen a couple of 'as soon as' slide right on by. We've applied for our visas. That still small voice is getting loud enough to listen to."

While I waited for Saguna, another much-loved friend, Vivek, left forever. Since the rebirth of the Poona commune our paths had seldom crossed. I heard she was deeply depressed and spent much of her time traveling. In the commune she chose to live in Krishna House rather than Lao Tzu, leaving the care of Bhagwan to Chetana and Anando. I never saw her on the paths or in the cafeteria.

But in White Robe she came alive, an explosion so vivid, so total—her heavy brown hair flying, her eyes wide and flashing, every particle of her body and being dissolved into the dance—I could only stare in delight.

One day I encountered her suddenly as she came through the gate. Her face was drawn and white, eyes wide and staring, like a mask. So helpless and lost did she look that I threw my arms around her, hugged her tight: "Vivecker!" For a moment she melted, smiled, hugged me back. Then her body grew stiff and drew away.

"Can we have coffee somewhere?" I asked, anxious to keep some contact, to help her through whatever horror had taken her over. But she shook her head.

"Ask me in a few days, Nirgie," she said with an attempt at a smile. "I'm not feeling so great, just need to be alone for a bit." And she was gone.

I never saw her again. Alarmed, I sought out Chetana, told her my fears. "Vivek looks like she's on the point of death. Is anyone keeping in touch with her?"

Chetana's face echoed my concern. "We're all trying, Nirgun," she said. "We call on her but she sends us away; says she's fine, just doesn't want visitors."

Three weeks later I heard Vivek had died from an accidental over-dose of sleeping pills. Her body was cremated the same night, with only a few close friends present.

I think her death was not accidental. Like me, she had known Osho's new bedroom for what it was: a samadhi.

Osho said, "Vivek died an untimely death."

January 16, 1990. Lively flutes and light, fast percussion rev up at the whisper of his car wheels on the marble driveway. A great flurry of drums . . . "Osho!" we shout, arms flung open to the skies. Again the burst of drums . . . "OSHO!" The avalanche of sound roars out into the night, the peacocks squawk and flutter from the trees. "OSHO—O—O—O!"

He enters namasteing, smiling, in a simple dark-azure robe, the panels outlined with white oval beads. We clap wildly, arms thrusting upward to the sky, a white sea of bodies in perpetual motion, ripples within ripples within ripples, like waves hit by a sudden squall.

Tonight he can't conduct us, his arms are too weak. That grim knowledge puts fresh energy into our mad dance.

Osho crosses the podium with infinite slowness, still facing us. His steps, always small, now seem minuscule. For long minutes his eyes search the vast expanse of the hall, front to back, seeking contact with each one. Ten rows back, still I know when he looks at me: the

Osho greeting sannyasins back in Poona .

same tingling in the solar plexus, the same steely rush of energy. I feel it piercing inside.

Osho reaches his chair and slowly seats himself; the music changes to soft sitar and flute. Buddha Hall is a pool of silence: stillness after the storm.

My body freezes into a solid block, unmoving, immovable. But now I am outside it, somewhere on the ceiling. Looking down, seeing Osho in his chair, startling blue on white. Seeing the still-life musicians, the drums, the flutes, the guitars, the vast hall of motionless white—*where am I?* In the same timeless moment I am back in my body, my hands still pressed together in namaste.

Osho brings his hands slowly upwards, beats with the back of his right hand very softly against the palm of his left, keeping time to the soft music. He stops suddenly; the musicians stop in the same instant.

A silence, then his hands begin to move again. The flute and guitar respond. Stop. Silence.

Three drumbeats, then lively music strikes up to send him on his way. But as he namastes us in his slow voyage across the stage he is not smiling. I sit on in the silence long after the car has whispered away.

The following night he comes to greet us but doesn't stay for the meditation.

The next night he doesn't come out at all.

On the evening of January 19, Buddha Hall overflows. The news of Osho's growing weakness has spread like a fire blown by the wind. I see sannyasins from around the world, just arrived; but no Saguna.

A flute sparkles, light and fast, against the driving beat of many drums. We dance on the spot, there is no room to move. Putting every ounce of our attention and energy into the dance, holding nothing back. As if by fierce effort, acting together, we can hold back the tide. My shout is a plea to the universe. "Osho!" "Osho! "Osho!"

The music stops. There is a vast and pregnant silence. Devaraj walks onto the podium and speaks into the sudden hush.

"I have an announcement to make," he says, his voice husky. "Osho has left his body."

I hear muffled screams, scattered cries of anguish, as if they are carried from another world. Where I am there is only vast quiet, calm. No thought, no feeling. Only a deep sense of rightness.

Devaraj continues, a light note in his voice, tears in his eyes.

"We asked him how we should celebrate his death and he said, 'You just take me to Buddha Hall for ten minutes and then take me off to the burning ghats.'" Ripples of laughter quickly fade.

"Let me just say to you that in death he was just as you would have expected: incredible." Devaraj is smiling now through his tears. "And when I started crying, he looked at me and said, 'No, no, that's not the way.'" In mock self-reproach he hits himself on the head with the microphone and the hall explodes with laughter.

"So let's give our master the send-off in death that's appropriate for someone who's lived his life as fully as any man ever has."

The musicians play. I dance full out, knowing he wants it so. Many are sobbing openly, but I don't feel any sadness. He wants to go, I have seen it in his eyes—wants to go back home, back to the source that is full of everything that is, or ever was, or ever will be.

Osho's simple bamboo pallet is carried in by his closest disciples. His body is serene in death as in life. The snow-white beard cascading down his chest highlights his unlined face.

The body is covered with a mass of greenery and flowers. Not formal wreaths but chain upon delicate chain of fragrant cream blooms, with dozens of huge fresh roses set in simple patterns. This is Mukta's work, I know. She has plucked every rose in his garden.

I turn inward. Wrapped in an inner silence so thick it lets in nothing but the music, I dance.

The inner silence gives way to an inner certainty, a certainty that takes form and shape, blossoms. *This is how I will go, dancing, celebrating. While I can still dance, still cut my own toenails! I won't wait to be dragged down by death in a stagnant old age. I'll just fling open the door myself with joy, anticipation—like opening the door to find my Christmas stocking. When I'm ready. I'll know the time.*

The certainty brings with it the delicious breeze of freedom.

My mind plays on. *Maybe I'll die like the cat in Osho's joke: get out the window, crawl up the rainspout and climb onto the roof!* My lips curl up in a soft smile at the memory of this hilarious death joke.

The road to the burning ghats is narrow, rutted, dark. The waning moon gives little light as thousands follow the flower-decked bier, the drums, the flute, the guitars. We come to a flat grassy space by the river. Sannyasins flood out in a great wave of white. I find a spot in the low branches of a tree. Enough light is there to glimpse the river eddying by, bearing its lavender clusters of floating water hyacinth.

Disciples cover the flower-decked body with blocks and chips, topping the wood with more flowers, leaving the face exposed.

Osho's eldest brother lifts a huge flaming torch. The funeral pyre bursts into uproarious life.

I am not conscious of grief. Fleeting glimpses of a reality beyond time and space have left me certain that the real Osho is not burning in this fire. But as I stare into the roaring flames consuming his beautiful, beloved form, tears pour down in a sudden fierce freshet of heartbreak.

He has talked to us of this moment. At daybreak I watch the graying embers that cradle his ashes, and from the depths of memory his words come back to me.

"When I am gone,
where can I go?
I will be here in the winds,
in the ocean.
If you have loved me,
if you have trusted me,
you will feel me in a thousand and one ways.
In your silent moments
you will suddenly feel my presence."

A morning breeze from the river touches my cheek, ever so gently.

In the afternoon a call comes from the front gate: "Saguna has come! He's waiting for you in the Welcome Centre."

His face is pale, his eyes are red-rimmed, full of tears; he knows. I grab him by the shoulders and give him a great shake.

"Hey, Saguna!" I tell him, my eyes sparking with fun. "There's something you've got to know. Yesterday Osho went kind of crazy. He somehow climbed out of the window! And damned if he didn't find a rainspout and start to crawl up it! And then he climbed out onto the roof. . . ."

Saguna listens at first with startled eyes and half-open mouth. Then his mouth slowly crinkles in a grin and we fall into each other's arms. Laughing. Crying.

Roundup Time

A ROUNDUP OF STRAYS—stray facts, ideas, hunches.
The fate of the Poona commune after Osho left his body can best be told with pictures and a few words from the media.

Osho Commune International exploded into the greatest spiritual and health center in the world:

> "Lushly landscaped . . . a spiritual Disneyland for disaffected First World yuppies . . . thousands of men and women pour through the gate every day, from Europe, America, Australia and Japan." (*The Wall Street Journal*).

> "Visit this remarkable ashram to see for yourself!" (*Vogue Magazine*).

> "Believers flock to 'Club Meditation'" (*The Oregonian*, printing a map of India to show its readers how to reach Poona.)

In India the once-persecuted Rajneesh is currently the country's bestselling author. His books are on display in the federal parliament library—an honor accorded to only one other, Mahatma Gandhi. Hilariously, he has been awarded the title of First Citizen by the City of Poona.

In the West, meditation has gone mainstream, and with it Osho's liquid religiousness—translated into 2000 titles in 44 languages—is flowing around the world. Even mainland China is publishing (and pirating) his works.

Sannyasins joke that the new information highway will soon double as a transformation highway: Four Web sites feature Osho, and now every discourse and video has been digitalized, ready to flash out on the new fiber-optic cables that big corporations are fighting to wire into every home on the planet.

These last years I've been leisurely writing this book, going to Poona for the winter months. The commune overflows with noisy celebration. Sannyasins digging into their psyche—falling from head to heart, from a lifetime of repression into free expression—are an exuberant lot. The burble of talk, songs and laughter fills the cafeterias, shops, bookstore, disco and walkways.

Celebration is basic to Osho's vision.

"What I am doing here is really giving people songs again, dances, changing the crosses into flutes," he told us in early Poona days. "My only desire is that every church starts singing, dancing, swinging!" This, he said, is a necessary first step. Only those flooding over with their own life energy are capable of knowing meditation, prayer, silence.

Celebration and meditation are the two wings of Osho's vision, but they may be growing out of sync.

"This commune will become a commune of silence," Osho told us in his last days, and I recall his unique definition of silence: "It is only man who creates noise. These birds, they sing silence; these trees, these rivers rushing toward the ocean, they sing silence. Yes, there is sound, but the sound has no noise in it. It is man who has brought word into existence, and through word he has become lost in the jungle of language." Music comes very close to meditation "because music is pure joy, festivity, it has no words . . . Today's music, singing, is almost insane."

New pyramid meditation halls at Osho Commune International in Poona, India, dubbed "Club Meditation" by the media.

Perhaps our kindergarten years have needed a strong accent on celebration. But I miss Osho's brand of festive silence. Years of working in the quiet space of his house—speaking only as needed, full attention on the task at hand, joy bubbling inside—have left a deep imprint on my psyche.

Even as I write, news comes from Poona that a vast new soundproof auditorium, part of Osho's vision, will be built in time for the Millennium Celebration in Poona.

"The building should rise out of the water," Osho told the Inner Circle. "Crossing the bridge will remind my people to leave the mind and go inside." The plans reflect his wishes.

And if the mind is truly left outside, words cannot enter.

What news of my sannyasin family? In 1993 Kaveesha and John, members of the Inner Circle, and David, also from the Hollywood set, returned to America. They founded the Osho Mystery School in Sedona,

Arizona, and all three live and work there, offering a broad program of groups and esoteric meditations. As in Poona, each day closes with the White Robe Brotherhood. Nirupa lives on her own in the foothills of the Himalayas. She travels the world, dropping in on friends and family and the Osho commune, exuding a quiet radiance. Saguna is rooted in Fremantle, West Australia, with a large juicy network of sannyasins; he comes to Poona most winters for groups and Zennis, I see him often. Turanti married a fellow sannyasin; both are taking graduate courses at university. When I visited two years ago they were still doing Osho meditations at home.

In Canada I stay grounded in my heart, in touch with my kids again. Every summer I pop into my Mazda and drive hundreds of miles to visit my non-sannyasin sons. And—joy of joys—Blair's daughter and son have come back into his life. Nancy comes to visit and keeps in touch by e-mail. Kelly, now a handsome twenty-one-year old, has moved from Vancouver, found a job, and now lives in a cabin on his father's quarter-acre. He and Blair share their delight in fixing old cars, playing in Christian rock bands, and making up for the years of separation.

My family grounds me in my heart, but my intellect needs food too; once an egghead, always an egghead. Writing this book has taken me into a strange world. I am fascinated by quantum mechanics, the branch of modern science that knocks the hell out of our ideas of time and space and common sense reality. That's just what Christ and Buddha, Socrates, Zen masters and Osho have been trying to do. All insist that our real self is inner and invisible. For the first time in human history, science is supporting spiritual insights.

Deepak Chopra M.D., renowned worldwide for his lectures and books on healing in the quantum world, describes our reality in enchantingly simple words:

"Your body appears to be composed of solid matter that can be broken down into molecules and atoms . . . But chasing the physical structure of the body down to its ultimate source dead-ends as molecules give way to atoms, atoms to subatomic particles, and these particles to ghosts of energy dissolving into an empty void . . . This void is mysteriously imprinted with information. The essential stuff of the universe, including your body, is non-stuff, but it isn't ordinary non-stuff. The void inside every atom is pulsating with unseen intelligence."

Experiments in quantum mechanics "prove that there is no underlying reality to the world," concludes John Gribbin, scientist and author. "Yet at the same time the fundamental particles that make up the universe seem to be connected into some indivisible whole, each aware of what happens to the others."

Quantum mechanics is "philosophically weird, conceptually contradictory, and often goes against our common sense," says Dr. M. Y. Chan in *The Probable Universe*. "A concept as basic as a thing occupying one fixed position at one moment of time is denied at the outset by the quantum world."

Eminent physicist John Wheeler of Princeton University has described our universe as 'observer-created'. "He means that the world does not come into being until a mind reacts with it . . . Bizarre though it seems, measuring the spin of one subatomic particle forces a twin particle, miles away, to have the opposite spin. The observer literally creates reality, much as Eastern and other holistic faiths teach." (From an article in *Newsweek*, November 8, 1994.)

So mysterious is the universe now glimpsed that many scientists are talking the language of the sacred, speaking with the same awe and reverence as mystics. Man can be seen as the apex of an infinite wave of intelligent energy that is reaching toward higher and higher realms of consciousness.

This new reality puts an end to all belief systems, to any idea of a clockwork universe invented by a static, omnipotent god. An "unseen intelligence" is at the core of all things. In meditation or silent prayer we can look inward, see clearly the urge to be superior, the narrow beliefs that divide us from our fellow man; get in touch with the inner intelligence, the "Kingdom of God" within, the spirit that unites us.

No more blind faith in mass movements—we can each hoist a sail, now and here, whenever the spirit moves us. Many solitary sails can harness the winds of change, bring us out of this ugly trough. And—who knows? Perhaps make this beautiful planet earth a lighthouse in our mysterious, unfolding universe.

In the long haul of eternity, there is no cause for alarm. If our model of homo sapiens chooses to self-destruct, another wave of creation will surely follow.

Existence is vast, and it has its own ways.

Writing these final words I am aware of a lightness, of the soft breeze of freedom. Next year my body will be seventy-five years old— five more than its Bible-allotted span of three score years and ten. Memory of recent events is clouding; toenails are thickening, hair thinning, the urge to create vanishing. Next year feels like a good time to drop out and go back to where I come from.

Scientists tell us that nothing in existence can ever go out of existence. Spiritual folk call it 'life eternal.' For me it's an inner certainty. Death can take the fading body, the static personality, the prickly ego— take them, and welcome. But it can't touch the infinite intelligence that throbs in every atom of our being.

Glossary of foreign and unfamiliar words

baba ~ respectful form of address to an older person
baksheesh ~ alms
Bhagwan ~ blessed one
brun ~ oval Indian bun
chapatis ~ bread dough rolled flat in a thin round and toasted
dahl ~ dish of lentils with aromatic fried spices
darshan ~ individual meeting with a master
deadhead ~ sunken log swept up by a fierce current
dhoti ~ long white loincloth worn by Indian men
dynamic meditation ~ catharsis and celebration
kundalini meditation ~ shaking, dancing
mala ~ wooden necklace worn by spiritual seekers
mali ~ gardener
moun ~ one who has taken a vow of silence
namaste ~ Indian greeting with palms together
Nadabrhama ~ meditation with humming and slow circular
    hand movements
Nataraj ~ dance as meditation
sammasati ~ Be total!
sannyas ~ accepting a master as your guide
tablas ~ two small drums
thali ~ silver or metal tray holding numerous small bowls
third eye ~ spot between the eyes, site of pineal gland, a vestigial
    organ of unknown function
Vipassana meditation ~ watching the breath; walking with awareness

Acknowledgments

To the sannyasins who appear in this book, I am deeply grateful: it could not have been written without their generous contribution of thoughts and feelings. My thanks go also to Pankaja and Tameer, who spent many hours digging out needed detail, and to Marga for her spontaneous support in a critical time. Very special thanks go to Amiyo Rain, M.D., whose passionate encouragement and tough, talented editing urged this fledgling book into robust life; to Sarlo, whose sly humor lightened our work; and to reader/commentators Rammurti, Vishram, and my son Saguna.

I am grateful to those who kept their homes and hearts open to me at all times, even when uneasy with the path I chose: my sons Blair and Craig, their wives Carol and Karen, Shirley and Manfred Schmid; to other friends who were always there in times of need—Shunya, Bernie, Cochlin, Peter and Pat Murray, Peter Stratton, Darlene Marzari, and computer wizard Norris of Broadway Radio Shack. And a special thank you to those early Gurdjieff teachers without whom this tale would not have been conceived: Ray "The Fake Sheik" Walker and E. J. Gold.

And finally, to my ebullient publisher Steven Scholl, whose enthusiasm reached out to snatch up this story of spiritual search and brought it to published life, with expert assistance from copy editor Sherri Emmons.

Grateful acknowledgment is given for use of material originally published by Osho Commune International, including transcribed discourses and darshan diaries from which all Osho quotes are taken. Acknowledged also is the verifying documentation gathered in Max Brecher's *Passage to India* and Juliet Forman's two books, *Twelve Days that Shook the World* and *Bhagwan: The Buddha for the Future*.